Journey into Joy

PRESS

A Superior Publishing Company

P.O. Box 115 • Superior, WI 54880
(715) 394-9513 • www.savpress.com

Journey into Joy

Jill Downs

First Edition

Copyright 2010, Jill Downs

First Printing
14 13 12 11 9 8 7 6 5 4 3 2 1

Cover Art: © 2010 Margaret Manderfeld

ISBN 13: 978-1-886028-91-3

Library of Congress Catalog Card Number: 2010929447

Published by:

Savage Press
P.O. Box 115
Superior, WI 54880

Phone: 800-732-3867
E-mail: mail@savpress.com
Web Site: www.savpress.com

Printed in the U.S.A.

Contents

Introduction

In *Journey Into Joy,* Jill explores her life in a series of episodes covering a wide range of topics, sharing her challenges, wisdom, humor, and joy, in hopes that others can benefit from her experience.

Peace

How can we be peaceful?
I once heard someone ask
The wise one answered,
"Finding peace within yourself
Must become your task."

How do I find peace within
When all the world's a mess?
The wise one said,
"Behold! These conditions you must bless."

How can I bless the hate, the fear
And all that isn't right?
"When you understand the purpose
You will see it in the Light."

How can I see the purpose
When I'm just a mortal soul in fear?
"You must open to your spirit
And the answer will be clear."

How do I open to the spirit?
How do I look inside?
"You must trust the God within yourself
And in His love abide."

And if I do this, will I know
Why the earth is full of pain?
"You will know this and more
For there's much for you to gain.

Yes, you will know just what to do
And you will see your part.
You will know how you can help
To ease the aching heart.

You will understand the seasons
And the reasons will be clear.
You will comprehend the cycles
And you'll know just why you're here.

You will know just when to speak
And what you are to say.
And you will know when silence
Proves to be the better way.

You will know when you should act;
You will know when to refrain;
You will understand through listening
There's much for you to gain.

You'll find that peace within yourself
That you've been longing for.
And you'll find the freedom you've been seeking
As you walk on through the door.

And when you're on the other side,
You'll know there is no fear.
You'll understand there's only love
And that is why you're here."

Letting Go

My childhood leaves me, for the most part, with fond memories and messages of love. I had a deep faith and was eager to please the people around me. I was fortunate to have a teacher in spirit who taught me to respond to life in joy rather than fear. She whispered in my ear that life was about learning. Thus, I saw my life as a series of lessons or tests that, if I trusted in God and myself, I would pass. I had an attitude of gratitude and life was about giving rather than receiving. I was generally happy and good-natured.

I remember being at the cabin in the late fall. My parents enjoyed hunting. We would get up very early—around 4:30 or 5:00 in the morning while it was still dark and chilly out. My mother made us breakfast. All of us, including my older brother and sister would get bundled up and walk the roads looking for partridge.

As children, in the evenings we often played games, including Monopoly. We ate popcorn and roasted marshmallows in the fire.

Wintertime in those early years was spent at our home in town. I have wonderful memories of skiing. I started skiing downhill in our backyard at the age of three. Later we were lucky to be able to go for the whole day to Mont du Lac, a popular ski hill in Wisconsin. Our good friends went with us. We skied all day and came home cold, exhausted and content.

Christmas time was indeed magical with memories of lots of presents, Christmas carols and fantasies of Santa Claus. (I'm sure I saw him in our living room. He always ate at least part of the snack we put out for him.)

Listening to the radio in the evenings was an important pastime in the '40s and '50s. I especially enjoyed *Our Miss Brooks*, *The Shadow*, and *The Lone Ranger*. However, my favorite was *Big Jon and Sparkie*, that aired at 8:00 on Saturday mornings. Part of the show was devoted to making sure that children tidied up their rooms for inspection, which was done by the magic magnifying glass. I would get up and scurry around cleaning up my room and then crawl back into bed and wait. Over the radio Big Jon would say things like, "Oh, I see little Johnny In Omaha, Nebraska, has socks under his bed." Hearing that I'd scramble out of bed and look underneath to see if I was safe. I didn't want <u>my</u>

name mentioned on the radio. People all over the country would hear I had a messy room.

Another part of the show was the Marching Band that called me out of bed once more to march around my room. The hardest thing was to stand up if I happened to be awake at midnight while my radio played the "Star Spangled Banner" signaling the end of the broadcast day.

Wintertime also brings with it memories of the ever-popular skating rink. As I became older, I spent hours there, both daytime and evening. We most often walked to and from the rink. When the streetlights came on, we knew it was time to come home—fingers freezing in wet mittens and our toes numb in our boots.

My parents always used to laugh whenever we drove past the skating rink. I'd scan the rink quickly which was packed with skaters and exclaim how, "Nobody was there," which meant of course, I saw nobody I knew or cared to skate with.

Springtime meant tulips growing in people's yards and Easter Sunday. As a child, I always had a new dress and shoes on Easter. Instead of just going to Sunday School that day, we got to go to church. The smell of spring always brought hope that the endless days of summer were on their way.

Summertime in the '40s and '50s meant playing outside all day. In those days dogs ran free and kids used their imaginations keeping themselves entertained until their parents called them home for supper. As I grew a little older, I was able to join the neighborhood baseball game that went on after dinner.

On Saturday mornings my friend and I had a little school that we created for a few of the small neighborhood children. Our school was held under a huge tree that was in our yard. We would go pick up the children in the morning and keep them occupied for a couple of hours with various activities until it was time to take them home. Their parents were grateful for our little school and encouraged us.

Summertime brought us also to the cabin, where, as a child, I particularly loved to swim. I think I was in the water more than I was out. We also had a sauna that was in a separate building from our cabin. I loved getting all hot and then running off the dock into the lake.

Summer in earlier years also meant going to Girl Scout Camp for two weeks each year. We were required to take tests at the end of our stay for boating, swimming and life saving. We also got to go to the P.X. and buy candy at special times. Receiving letters from home was always a joy. We'd read our mail during rest time in the afternoon.

As a young teenager, summers at the cabin were glorious. I had two friends—boys from my class at school whom I greatly enjoyed spending time with. Our parents were friends, as well. We spent day after day boating, waterskiing, canoeing, swimming and playing tennis until school started in the fall.

I greatly enjoyed my grade school years. I attended a wonderful school and was fortunate to have a class where I enjoyed friends, not only during school, but outside the classroom as well.

In the 7th and 8th grades some of us attended a ballroom dancing class that was held at the Country Club. It was fun and helped give us confidence and much to talk about as our parents drove us to and from the class.

Grade school in the '50s was a happy time for me. In general I loved myself, and those around me. I held high principles and lived up to the standards and values I'd set for myself while I had faith in my Creator as well as in myself.

Following grade school, which went up to the eighth grade, I spent one year at a Catholic girls' school. I was not Catholic, but it was "the place to go" if you wanted a good education. I wasn't particularly happy there and in the tenth grade, I went to Westover, a private girls' school in Connecticut. My mother and sister and a few other friends had also attended there.

I was just fourteen as I flew off to boarding school. My parents had given me a choice. I could have chosen to attend the high school where most of my friends were, but I decided, somewhat reluctantly, to take the opportunity to go away.

My years at Westover were actually rather uneventful. I enjoyed the Glee Club and was invited to sing with a smaller group called the Undertones. We traveled once to Philadelphia to sing for a gathering of alumni and for a lark, we sang at Grand Central Station in New York. I studied hard at Westover and remained true to myself.

Following my years at Westover, I chose to go to college. I had two great roommates and many friends at the coed dorm where I resided at the University of Minnesota, Minneapolis. However, I began to lose my sense of self and to become somewhat depressed and anxious regarding the complexities of life and my role in it. I started to enjoy the soothing effect of alcohol at social events and began to feel inferior, as I looked at others who seemed more "together" and confident. Instead of seeking help, which I don't remember ever occurring to me, I grew inward without sharing my feelings. After all, I'd been an expert at handling my life in the past.

Following two and a half years of college, my parents, sensing my "unhappiness" offered to send me to France for a period of time to live in a French family. My father had a business acquaintance who informed him of a wonderful family that was open to having a guest in their home.

Madame and her four children ages 17 to 6 welcomed me into their home, which was a lovely apartment in the 17th arrondissement of Paris. I have never regretted my experience. I went to a language school there, learned French and enjoyed touring the city on foot taking in all the sights and sounds of Paris.

However, much of the time was spent alone and I continued to enjoy the numbing effect of alcohol through the wine that was readily available. My family followed the European tradition of serving wine at both lunch and dinner.

After six and one half months in Paris, I began to have a longing for more structure in my life as well as a need to be of service. I decided to go into LPN training at the University of Minnesota in Minneapolis.

I was president of my class and enjoyed my studies as well as the practical work at the hospital. I later went to work at Abbott Hospital in Minneapolis. By that time I began to develop a fear around alcohol, as it was becoming more of an issue in my life.

In 1966 a family friend and Senator asked me if I would like to be a Page in the Minnesota State Senate. At that time I was dating my husband, Tony, and he encouraged me to take the opportunity. It was a fun job and I met many interesting people. It was also a party time with frequent dinners out with friends while the cocktails flowed freely.

I met my husband, Tony, at a party in Duluth. Two years later we announced our engagement and had a beautiful Christmas wedding in December of 1967.

Tony was finishing law school at the University of Minnesota and we lived in an apartment in Minneapolis where I went to school working toward my degree in sociology. I became pregnant and following Tony's graduation, we moved to Duluth. We were thrilled with the birth of our daughter, Cindy. Tony went to work in a law firm and I remained at home. Two years later we were blessed with the birth of our second daughter, Leila. It was a happy time.

For many years, with the children in the hands of a competent and loving baby sitter, weekends were spent partying with good friends and staying out late. We went to each other's homes for dinner and went out on the town. We went on hunting, fishing and camping trips. We took trips to the Bahamas with a dear friend and enjoyed a trip to South America with another couple. We truly had some wonderful times. However, I was becoming attached to alcohol, which later became more of a problem for me.

My daily life included playing the role of mother to our two young daughters whom I loved dearly. However, beyond caring for our children, I was anxious and depressed. We had the birthday parties. I took the girls to their doctor and dentist appointments and made sure they learned how to swim, ski and skate. I tried to be a good mother. However, much of the time I isolated myself—staying in the house as neighborhood gossip didn't appeal to me nor did belonging to clubs and organizations.

Feeling sorry for myself, I hadn't yet discovered the joy of living in the Light. I chose instead the hard way to love and care for myself. Naps in the afternoon were frequent as I was exhausted and drinking was a part of every day life as I had yet to view my challenges as opportunities for growth.

I wasn't living up to my ideals so any kind of prayer to my Creator felt empty. In my mind I felt undeserving. As time went on, lapses in memory were occurring with the remorse that followed. I was consumed with guilt and badly needed help with the crisis I was in. In my every day life I was trying to fit in. At one point I went to school and was taking a difficult course in statistics that miraculously I did well in. My drinking continued. I had difficulty sleeping and was exhausted physically and emotionally.

As time went on, I totally lost my sense of self. I was filled with frustration, anger and resentment mostly at myself for not honoring my values and gifts. I had ceased to believe in myself and lacked the courage and ability to speak up for my needs and concerns. Panic attacks were frequent. I was jealous and insecure.

I thought of getting help, but didn't know where to turn. I suspected I was an alcoholic, yet the thought of treatment scared me and living without alcohol was not enjoyable. I was in trouble and I knew it.

One evening in November of 1980, Tony made the wise decision to make arrangements to get me into treatment. I was frightened and in despair. However, once there, and settled in, I was relieved and in peace with my choice to stay and complete the program. I am aware that at pivotal times in our lives, when important decisions need to be made, high guidance comes in to direct us. Love for myself, concern for my family and my health helped me in my choice to remain in the care of professionals.

My former life being dissolved and obstacles removed, I placed myself in God's hands, adapting well to treatment and enjoying the friendships I made there. Treatment was a transforming experience for me. I came to understand that my alcoholism was only a symptom masking feelings that needed to be uncovered, brought to light and healed, as well as issues to be resolved.

I felt guilt and shame for having ended up in this situation. Being an alcoholic was the last thing I ever dreamed of "happening to me." However, I was encouraged by others who felt similarly—individuals who held high standards for themselves—and found it difficult to comprehend how they got to where they were in their lives. Yet eventually we learned to laugh at our predicament and not take ourselves so seriously—a good lesson that I take to heart today.

While in rehab, I began to see letting go as a process that would be with me for as long as I'm alive on this earth. I learned it was important to feel my emotions without fear, to honor their place in my life and then let them go.

I learned that in order to have peace, I must turn my worries and cares over to my Higher Power. Further, I learned to take responsibility for my own thoughts, feelings, and actions without blaming others for my difficulties or my past.

Living in the Light without alcohol meant making the choice to live without inner turmoil and drama. It was essential I learn to stand up for myself, trust in Divine Intelligence and express my truth without fear. Learning once again to believe in myself was, and sometimes still is, a powerful lesson for me.

Upon returning home I began loving my new life and meeting new people also in recovery. One day a good friend of mine asked me if I cared to join him and his wife at the First Spiritualist Church that is now called the Lake Superior Interfaith Community Church. They had just recently started attending services there. I agreed and was overjoyed with my experience. Rev. Hutchinson was the minister and was also a medium. I loved the church and got involved in all of its activities. I came to enjoy most of all the mediumship aspect of the church service wherein divine messages full of hope and encouragement were lovingly delivered by Rev. Hutchinson to some of those in attendance. I also enjoyed his meditation class during which time gifts were explored while messages in the Light were received by those of us in the class and given out in the group. I went on to lead Rev. Hutchinson's meditation class following his retirement and also served as board president of our church. Further, as a result of my training by Rev. Hutchinson and others, as well as inspiration coming to me from my own life experience and divine intelligence, I created and led workshops in the community on personal and spiritual growth.

In December of 1992 I had a spontaneous Kundalini experience—or spiritual awakening followed by a long period of healing that included further journeys into consciousness. This process required me to live in two worlds at once. I was enjoying the astral plane or "spirit realm" while doing my best to be present on earth.

Suffice it to say, I felt very much alone during that time. My adventure was a mission I regarded as sacred. I chose not to talk about it because there were no words to adequately convey all that I experienced. It was a great gift and I felt honored to undergo all that I did, even though parts of it were indeed challenging and even frightening. However, where there is darkness, there is also Light, and I couldn't begin to express the joy, love, and miraculous events that surrounded me. It was difficult to "come down" and just carry on like nothing had happened. To say the experiences were extraordinary wouldn't touch the essence. I was blessed, indeed. I am truly grateful to my husband and daughters for their supporting me as best they could while there was no way they could comprehend what I was experiencing.

As a result of my inner experiences, I accomplished many goals, which included facing and dealing with unconscious fears while releasing old patterns and healing wounds of the past. It became necessary to discern the real from the symbolic as well as the meaning of the spiritual and religious symbolism with which I was presented.

Clarity and intent in regard to channeling was and still is a constant source of enlightenment to me as I learn to love and honor all aspects of myself. I was honored and delighted to experience and travel the astral plane. My awareness of being supported and guided by the Master Jesus and other divine beings greatly aided my journey.

As a result of my experiences on the inner planes, I gained a renewed sense of self and corresponding life. The turmoil had ended and I felt safe and secure as I always was in God's hands.

Due to my spiritual awakening, I now live with an attitude of forgiveness and faith in myself, and others. I am no longer impatient with my growth as I see myself, and my challenges in the Light. I have faith in my Higher Power and am learning to trust in myself. I enjoy the astral plane but no longer "live there." I am grounded and at peace with my family and friends.

Previous to my Kundalini awakening and journeys into consciousness, I had a picture in my mind about where my life was going. I had plans for myself wherein I would be of service using my skills as a medium and a teacher. It was a plan that seemed perfect for me and I was looking forward to it. However, as time went on, my future became a blur—yet I was content. I began to rediscover myself through letting go of the past and waking up to the beauty around me.

Little did I know that once I let go of my original plans and allowed time to heal, that that which would come to me was much more fulfilling, beneficial, and joyful than I ever dreamed possible. I now cherish my alone-time and live in my heart. I enjoy life to the fullest and feel truly blessed.

During my time of healing I became aware that some challenges take longer to heal than others. But each time an issue comes around I become aware that I have the opportunity to respond in the Light to the challenge.

Anger and resentment posed a big problem for me at a particular time in my life. As a child, I rarely got angry. Therefore, much anger was stored from an earlier time. I also believe I brought in, on a soul level, the anger issue to heal from previous lifetimes. Whether one believes in reincarnation or not, is irrelevant here. The issues are there to heal regardless of their origin.

One evening I was suffering through a particular resentment I was carrying and I happened to notice on top of our TV, a very small white Bible. This was a little Children's Bible I'd had since I was a child. I did not recall bringing this up from the bookshelf in the basement, but there it was. I couldn't believe it when I saw it turned over face down on top of the TV. The place marked was the 13th chapter of Corinthians, which is all about love. I knew then my answer was about love and forgiveness. There was no one in the house responsible for placing the Bible where I found it. So this was my little miracle. I've never forgotten it. This is not the only time I've witnessed things disappearing and reappearing in odd places. Our Higher Power is definitely in charge.

Letting go of worry and fear has been another big challenge for me. Once again I found myself in God's hands in spite of myself. One night I was having difficulty sleeping as I had decided instead to put myself through hours of worry and fear about a certain situation when in actuality there was nothing to be upset about. I heard a loving voice say, "You're fine and there's nothing to worry about." I had trouble believing it. Finally, I heard the voice say, "Go into the porch and watch TV. It will distract you." I went into the porch and lay down on the couch but didn't turn on the TV as, of course, that might interfere with my worrying. Finally, while I was lying there torturing myself with my negative thoughts, the television went on by itself. I got the message. All was indeed well and I was protected and in good hands. Sometimes God has to go to great lengths for me to get the point.

Learning to love myself in spite of my foibles and idiosyncrasies has taken time. Having compassion, patience and allowing myself to learn while following my own path and my own timing, has been challenging, yet rewarding. There's always the temptation to compare oneself to others. Whenever I would engage in that kind of thinking, I would hear, "But you're on a different path." That always gratified me because I would have a tendency to feel left behind or as if somehow I had missed the boat. I hadn't. Believing in myself and having the courage to follow my own intuition has been of utmost importance. Had I not followed my heart I would not be accomplishing my goals, which are bringing me greater love, peace, joy, and responsibility than if I'd chosen another path. Therefore, in letting go of where I thought my life was going, I trusted in my judgment and my Higher Power and gratefully let go and let God.

My life used to be quite busy. I always thought it was important, even vital, for me to be "doing something." I was very active in our church. I volunteered, presented my workshops, took classes in the community or I went to school. The thought of doing none of these things never occurred to me. In those days I think it was important that I was busy. However, I realize now that part of that was feeling that I needed to be accomplishing something in order to please God or to be able to love myself. Following my Kundalini experience and resulting journeys into consciousness, my awareness changed. I discovered life was more about "being" than necessarily about "doing." During this period I really learned to let go.

Thankfully, I released the need to "accomplish" or prove myself either to myself, or others. I have learned to have greater acceptance and patience with the things I wish to change within myself and have gained greater knowledge and wisdom as a result of becoming honest with who I am at a deeper level than was previously possible. Further, I've gained greater love and understanding of myself, and others as I learned to trust in the process of healing and growth to which we all aspire. Also, I've found greater peace in learning to trust, through all the turmoil inherent in my adventures in the infinite intelligence that lies within us all.

The Challenge in Living in The Light

The challenge is learning to "be."
To join the commotion
—The rat race in motion
Is natural and easy for me.

The challenge is living the Light.
—Running and doing,
—Worrying and stewing.
It's tempting to put up a fight.

The challenge is in "letting go."
To live and just "be"
Is not easy for me.
What's easy is running the show.

Surrender is not what it seems.
We know the reward that it means,
Yet we persist and still we insist
That doing it our way fulfills dreams.

There's wisdom in learning to "be."
There's comfort in learning to see.
It's not what we do, but who we are, too,
That's important to you and to me.

Take time to enjoy your day.
See your life in a whole new way.
Discover your gifts and know there exists
Much more that is hidden away.

Take time to honor your "being."
Know there's more to you than you're seeing.
Be kind to yourself, take care of your health,
And know that your soul you are freeing.

Forgiveness

Forgiveness is the key that unlocks the door to self-realization and it's only as I forgive others that I feel forgiven.

Communicating with others during my meditation time helps me. I invite in those souls to whom I need to make amends. I summon them in love and Light and discuss the issue while asking for forgiveness. Sometimes those with whom I engage speak to me. Rarely do I have difficulty with friends and loved ones not accepting an apology. At other times, where appropriate, making amends to people on the physical level is beneficial.

Looking back on some difficult times when I was using alcohol, I wish I'd been a better mother. However, in my heart I know I was doing the best I could at the time.

Fortunately, both Cindy and Leila successfully met the challenges they were faced with and turned out to be women whom I admire and of whom I'm extremely proud. They are both individuals with great courage, strength and kindness. They are intelligent, humorous, fun and I adore them. There is indeed a God who watches over all of us!

I'm forever grateful to my husband, Tony, for the wonderful lessons and growth he has brought me throughout the years. I'm especially thankful for our trips we take each year, which he so generously arranges for us as well as for the care he takes in providing for his family. He is in my heart always and deserves special attention for his bright mind, sense of humor, and the joy he brings to me. He remains forever my friend and I love him dearly.

There was a time earlier in my life when I thought I would break apart if I allowed my feelings to surface. From that point of view alcohol was my salvation—a pattern, I believe, I brought into this lifetime to heal.

Thankfully, with the help of others and my divine healers in the spirit realm, I was able to set alcohol aside and began to have the courage to feel again, as well as forgive myself for not living up to my ideals.

If someone had told me early on that I would become an alcoholic, I would not have believed them. Like many with the disease, I was a perfectionist in ways and held high standards for myself.

Forgiving myself began with becoming honest with who I was. It also involved airing resentments, releasing self-pity and fear, while learning once again to believe in myself. Thank God, however, for joy in recovery. Recovering alcoholics can be very humorous people and often have the ability to laugh at themselves. Within this community I have sustained many long-standing friendships.

I was also given a new perspective on spiritual growth until which time my prayer being answered, I acquired my own spiritual philosophy, heightened awareness, and made the decision to follow my own heart. Nevertheless, forgiving myself didn't come easily. I eventually understood that being kind to myself was important and that forgiving any past mistakes and indiscretions was essential. I used to judge myself too harshly but I now understand I needed certain experiences to help me to grow and become all I was meant to be.

I can honestly say that I am truly grateful for my past. It has given me compassion for myself and the ability to help others see the Light within themselves.

Forgiveness is needed as well for not always seeing myself in the Light on various issues that arise for my healing. Like the peeling of an onion, each new layer is met with a challenge to see if, this time, the opportunity will be taken to alter the pattern.

Love for myself and a gentler approach to my human frailties is replacing a history of self-criticalness. My yoga routine in particular teaches me to be gentle and patient with my body. I am learning to accept myself where I am, right now, with the knowledge that tomorrow my yoga practice may be more enlightened.

I am more forgiving of my mistakes as well. Rather than judging my thoughts, I'm learning to observe and release them. Being consciously on a spiritual path, I am aware that the path narrows as I grow. There is, therefore, a temptation to become more self-critical. That is a road I choose not to take. Learning to forgive my mistakes, maintain a sense of humor and find joy in my life is my preferred path to a Light-filled existence.

I need also to forgive myself for not always seeing others in the Light. It's truly wonderful how people act as mirrors for us showing us things about ourselves we'd rather not see.

Observing someone's need to control their circumstances, or other people, reminds me of my own desires and tendencies. Judging myself will only bring the situation around again because loving and forgiving myself are the lessons to be learned. Therefore, I need only be aware of it when the thoughts arise, observe myself and others with compassion and let it go. The pattern is then released when I've learned to see it in the Light.

Along with forgiving myself I need to forgive my family and all who contribute directly and indirectly to my growth and enlightenment. Several years ago on a sizzling hot summer day my husband, Tony, and I were walking the "Lake Walk" as it's called, being adjacent to Lake Superior. Due to the excessive heat, I began to feel symptoms of heat exhaustion, which frightened me somewhat, as we had some distance to go to the restaurant where we intended to sit and relax. We had left a car there earlier so we could drive home.

I mentioned to Tony that I was somewhat dizzy and not feeling well. I managed to make it to the restaurant without incident and we had a beverage to quench our thirst. I'd been rather hoping he might ask me if I needed to go to the hospital, as he had been quite concerned. Leaving the restaurant we got into our car and Tony started heading up the hill toward the mall. He stated he needed to go to Lenscrafters. I said to him, in my disappointment at his failure to read my mind, "I didn't know Lenscrafters had an emergency room." We had a good laugh about that and since then it's been a joke between us.

Forgiveness of others who lacked the understanding to view me in the Light on my spiritual awakening and subsequent journeys into consciousness took patience and courage. I truly felt that my process was in the Light, yet not all of my experiences were "Light-filled." Indeed some were extremely challenging and frightening and although I received periodic assistance from various wonderful and gifted intuitive healers, I felt alone. However, I always knew I was protected and surrounded by divine love.

In retrospect I can see how others around me would be concerned as I was very often distracted living both in the spirit world and on earth. Caught between two worlds, I appeared not to be present, which was, in fact, true.

My friends and family were frightened and saddened that I was not myself and needed outside help. With the assistance of a wonderful and understanding psychiatrist, and others in the physical world, as well as divine help from God and my healers in the spirit realm, my energy soon stabilized and I made a speedy recovery.

I also believe strongly that it was my love for myself, my determination to honor my intuition and my process that gave me the strength to get grounded and pursue my goals.

I felt extremely gratified by my wondrous experiences, which gave me insight into myself as well as great joy. It opened me up to the spirit world, to other Light-Beings as well as to different levels of consciousness and a heightened awareness. I was shown how to navigate the astral plane in safety and was in delight with my experiences.

I do not judge myself for my travels into the realm of spirit, as I know it was part of my path and was blessed by my Higher Power. I was guided always by the Master Jesus, the angels, archangels, and other divine beings.

As a result of my journey and subsequent healing, I now trust in God and know I am in divine protection always. Further, I am determined to enjoy my life and to assist others in their own healing.

In spite of my experiences and inner awareness the universe still humors me with conditions and situations that challenge me to stay in the Light. The slow driver ahead of me; the person with too many items in the fast lane at the grocery store; the elderly lady with a handful of coupons at the checkout counter all call for a general attitude of forgiveness. When these types of events pop up in my day, I realize I need to slow down and remind myself that I am not in charge.

I need also to forgive others who appear to stand in the way of my goals. It is with love and amusement that I now observe the challenges, which I understand I've created for myself in order to grow.

Staying in the Light and following my heart are lessons I've chosen to learn in this lifetime. What greater reward could I have than to be clairaudient, which means I hear voices from the spirit realm. I recognize this is indeed a gift, but to be honest, it is, for me, a huge challenge as well.

Learning discernment concerning the voices is an on-going issue for me. I must decide where the voices are coming from, if they are in divine Light and who is speaking to me. While later, as part of my process, I needed to learn, as best I can, to follow my own heart and intuition.

Those in spirit who are my guides and helpers often give me "Lessons in the Light" involving decisions I must make. My challenge is to make the choices which are the most empowering and Light-filled for me.

It is my joy to connect with spirit friends as I receive much divine love and wisdom that can benefit me as well as others. I am aware the Master Jesus and other enlightened beings are always with me with their constant love and protection. They assist me in understanding my challenges and help me to love myself unconditionally while honoring my process and staying in my heart.

Forgiveness is needed as well for those with whom we share our lives. Petty annoyances, grave disappointments and resentments, as well, can be debilitating and all-consuming. For me, understanding the effects of past lives, though not a necessity, helped me greatly when I was in a crises and didn't understand why my life seemed so difficult, painful and confusing. I was most grateful to be given pictures through my intuition of an earlier lifetime, which explained a great deal to me and helped me to understand my present predicament.

I believe we are continually balancing that which occurred previously while learning to heal our patterns. I know that the wheel of karma need not continue when I choose to live in the Light. In my enlightened awareness my fears are released while self-pity is no longer part of my nature. Anger and resentment are in the past and I accept with gratitude the gifts that living without judgment give me.

Friends

Some friends are forever,
And some come and go.
All friends are there
To help us to grow.

Some friendships are easy,
And some can be fun.
Others are painful,
We may choose to run.

But one thing's for sure.
If we run astray,
A new friend will come
To show us the way.

Our lessons through others
We cannot escape.
New friends keep coming,
Our lives to help shape.

Some act as mirrors
Our reflections we see.
I look at you
And yet I see me.

What is it about you
That irritates me?
What is there hidden
That I cannot see?

People who bother us
Day after day,
Have come to help us
To show us the way.

Let me be aware
Of what needs to be healed.
There's something within me
That's been concealed.

I know if I look
Hard and long in my mirror,
My friend will soon show me
Why she is here.

What is my challenge—
My lesson with you?
I send out a prayer
So I know what to do.

Help me to know,
Allow me to see.
What is it about you
That draws you to me?

The angel I call
No need to be frightened.
I ask for awareness—
To be enlightened.

The angels respond
Through my intuition.
Enlightenment comes,
My prayer bears fruition.

Oh, now I see
What it is I must do.
Now I understand
Why I am with you.

Accepting the truth
Can be a relief.
A reason for sure
To change my belief.

About this mirror
Standing before me.
About this challenge
To be all I can be.

This one has come
To help me to grow.
Freedom at last
Because now I know.

With the help of angels
From the beyond
That I can change
How I respond.

So I thank my friend
Who was sent to me,
And I thank the angels
For setting me free.

Loving Yourself

One of my goals in this life is to learn to love and accept all aspects of myself at any given time. A tall order, I know, but through honoring my process and following my heart, I know I can succeed.

Loving and accepting myself was easy, for example, when I was active in my church. The challenge began when I chose to simply attend the church solely for the purpose of enjoying the service and the people without guilt while still honoring myself and my path. It was a hard lesson for me because it had been instilled in me, as it was in many of us, that we must be accomplishing something or be "busy" in order to be loved my our Higher Power, let alone ourselves.

Very often I have a voice that tells me I should "pitch in and help" or that I should give the talk at church (our church has guest speakers each Sunday), or facilitate the healing service—all of which I know I'm capable. However, I have been reluctant because my discernment tells me that this voice is coming from my mind and not my heart. It's an old voice—the voice that says I should be accountable to others. I need to let go of that old song and respond instead to that which comes from a loving heart and joyous intention.

I do enjoy clearing the table sometimes following our luncheon downstairs after the service. Again, I listen to my heart and if I feel resistance, I let it go. I don't judge myself for doing what I want to do.

This lesson for me is about learning to live with joy. At an earlier time in my development the challenge was all about exploring my abilities, talents and creativity with others. Therefore, being "out there" and taking part in church activities was meaningful, appropriate and beneficial for me.

For many years now I've being challenged with the lesson of learning just to "be" and also to enjoy my life. To do things for no other reason than pure enjoyment, I needn't prove anything to myself or to others and I can love myself for who I am as a child of God and not for anything I do or do not do. I enjoy reading novels, which is something I never thought about doing a number of years ago. I used to feel I needed to be learning something or "doing" something. I'm glad and grateful for the change. I'm still in the process of learning to relax and simply enjoy my life.

Loving myself also has to do with having compassion for myself. I have a spirit guide who constantly reminds me when I'm being too hard on myself which is more times than I care to admit. However, as with everything else, I have great faith in the process of my life and know I'm learning my lessons "on time."

I had an experience having to do with compassion with my palm plant that moved me to tears. The plant hadn't been doing well. I had bought it from Wal-Mart and it wasn't too healthy when I took it home. But at one point, it started to go down hill. I talked to it telling it I understood and that if it wanted to die, I would bless it and let it go. I continued giving it loving care and within a very short time, it was more than alive and well. It was beaming!

This reminded me not only that plants have feelings and respond to love and Light, it taught me about having compassion for myself as well as patience with my growth and healing. It reminded me also that, to the extent that I tend to the Light within myself, I will be able to have compassion for others.

Along this journey toward self-awareness I've also learned to release the need to compare myself with others. We have different paths at different times but I believe we all get the same lessons and challenges at one time or another over a series of lifetimes. None of us is exempt.

At times when we glance over at our friends and acquaintances to see what they're doing, we can feel mystified either at how easy or difficult someone's life appears to be. Comparing our life to that of another is like comparing apples and oranges. We're all in different places learning different lessons and healing diverse patterns at various times.

The challenge has been to love myself through my healing. A few summers ago two of my friends and I took a training course in rowing. We were seated in long boats that carried approximately ten of us. I'd done a lot of boating as a teenager out at our cabin and had wonderful memories of that time. This was different. I did all right but it was a bit stressful for me as I have a hearing problem and listening to the commands and directions is a large part of the sport. To make a long story short we entered a regatta following the course. I had misgivings because I felt we might be required to be in a boat with experts as there were no beginner boats lined up. I stressed about it and finally withdrew from the competition. I was happy with myself because I allowed myself to follow my heart and not feel like a failure. I vowed I would encourage my friends and cheer them on without feeling badly about myself. As it turned out none of us were in the race. There apparently "wasn't room for us" and I believe we were all relieved. As for me, I feel a lesson in loving myself was learned.

I used to feel unhappy about certain conditions in my life that I am now able to see in the Light. For example, I used to feel guilty and ashamed if I had negative spirits around me. I placed great judgment upon myself and had difficulty seeing myself in the Light.

At one time I had a troublesome entity with me whom I allowed to cause much fear and anxiety within me. However, when I realized this being had no power over me and I was able to let go of my fear and raise my vibration, the negative energy was released. It is my belief that we all have negative energies that come to help us heal our patterns. However, it is when we see, feel, or hear these energies more directly, that we can be frightened and overwhelmed beyond belief, until we understand that love is the answer to our dilemma.

Looking back I can see the purpose behind all that "happened to me" on an energy level, whether it was in the physical or spiritual realm and understand it is a lesson in loving myself and staying in the Light. I keep reminding myself that, "It is all a play—a drama. Observe yourself and stay in the solution as best you can." Learning to be patient with myself, honoring my process and learning to love myself has helped me to release all that doesn't serve.

Many of my lessons come through my relationship with the spirit world. I am extremely sensitive and clairaudient which means, as I explained earlier, that I hear spirit voices. I spent many years in Rev. Hutchinson's meditation classes where we learned to give spirit messages to others, as well as led classes of my own. Several years later my friends took courses in mediumship and went on to become ministers. However, I knew that route was not for me. Instead, much to my benefit, I both struggled and enjoyed astral traveling, led by the Master Jesus, on my own.

This was my main tool for self-discovery and healing not to be recommended to anyone unless being told to do so by their inner conscience and divine being. So while others were learning their lessons out there in the world, I was getting mine—mostly on the inner planes.

It has indeed been both a challenge and a delight living in two worlds at once.

I would, for example, become aware that one or both of my deceased parents were there with me in spirit and I would sometimes acknowledge my inner child's need for approval. I wanted their acceptance and love. If, however, I were in a high vibration at the time with my own self worth intact, their visit wouldn't throw me off balance and would bring only joy to me.

Occasionally negative spirits with ill intentions would impinge on my space. This had the potential to catch me off guard and elicit within me either anger, fear, or both. However, happily, this no longer has an effect on me. I call on the Master Jesus, Archangel Michael and my angels, and send love to the misguided spirit. At other times I ask God for help and the spirit is removed—the most important thing being to stay in the Light.

Self-respect and honoring my values are continuing issues for me as I coexist consciously with the spirit world. There are those beings and entities who do whatever they can to discredit or diminish those of us who are Light workers. My lesson has been to stay in the Light no matter what is happening in the astral, and shut the door where my identity, self-respect, or values are being compromised. This has been a monumental task, but the benefits and rewards derived from learning the necessary discernment have been greatly beneficial.

To remain in balance is very important in my day-to-day life. I have a tendency to enjoy being alone but I often have to remind myself how much I also love being with my friends. Friendships are very significant and nourishing for me. I derive a great deal of pleasure especially from one-on-one contacts with my friends. My husband and I also enjoy couples that we see often.

I regularly spend time during the day communing with loving spirits who are in the Light. They bring me solace, joy, love, support, and, thank God, humor!

Learning to give to myself in one way or another has been an important and beneficial lesson for me. There were times in my life when I was both acknowledged and praised for my gifts.

Throughout my growing up years from grade school through college and beyond, I'd held numerous leadership positions. During my forties when I was president of our church board, I enjoyed compliments from others concerning my work with individuals as well as groups. People seemed to enjoy my workshops as well as my book, *The Awakening of the Heart*, and I felt both honored and privileged to be a part of it all.

Later on as my life evolved, I chose to work on myself at deeper levels. This required setting my work aside in order to benefit from the lessons and challenges that were necessary in learning to truly understand myself.

During this time, as I noticed the compliments stopped coming and the praise dwindled for something I'd written or said in a workshop, I felt the loss. Where were the kudos? I missed the acknowledgment. However, fortunately I understood the opportunity.

I needed to learn self-reliance. I needed to learn to give the praise I wanted from others to myself. I chose to companion myself through difficult times—to learn how to be my own best friend. It was important I learn not to abandon myself but support myself through the uneasy transition from being a more public person to one who greatly cherishes a private life.

There are times when loneliness for whatever reason can be an issue, as I believe it is for all of us. I may think it's a friend in the physical or even the spiritual realm I'm longing for, but in reality I'm needing to connect with my soul. It is at these times it's good for me to be creative in some way that suits me, or perhaps it's journaling that can help bring me in touch with my Higher Self. Listening to music, reading and yes, even watching TV at certain times under certain conditions, can alleviate a feeling of loneliness and bring balance to my being.

I'm eternally grateful for my great abundance and joy. I'm aware I have the power through God to create a life that is wondrous and magical. By making the enjoyment of my life a priority, I come into contact with beings both in the physical and spiritual realm who support my dreams and assist me in fulfilling my wishes and desires.

I love the evenings on our deck overlooking Lake Superior with the warm balmy summer breezes. As I sit in solitude in my comfortable chair, I look out and enjoy the moon and its golden reflection on the still water. I love watching the ore boats and foreign ships that seem to appear out of nowhere, skimming across the surface of the lake with their lights twinkling like diamonds. Out of the corner of my eye, I see a fox coming out of the woods onto our lawn. It looks straight ahead as it faces off with a fat raccoon that boldly claims its territory. I look up to see a single star shining brightly in the evening sky with the assurance that indeed all is well.

I am overcome with love and gratitude as I witness my surroundings and count my blessings. It is in this environment that I feel moved to send out prayers and healing for others. I connect with my Higher Power, draw in divine Light, and send love while asking for the highest good for whomever I'm sending healing to, including also any messages that I'm inspired by God to give them.

It's healthy for me to send love and healing because it helps bring balance to my energy. When I am aware of being in such a great state of abundance, I know it is wise to send help and loving thoughts to others. It sets me free to continue to enjoy all the divine gifts the Creator has bestowed upon my family and me.

In the winter months I sit on my favorite chair in our living room. I listen to soft healing music and light several candles that remind me that I'm in a sacred space that is both protective and nourishing.

I use my aromatherapy which helps me to feel calm and cleansed. My heart becomes full as I contemplate my life and surroundings and all I've been blessed with. I call on God, Jesus, and other divine beings to assist me. Each moment is special as I use God's energy to reach to family and friends who have difficulties. I rest assured in the knowledge that they will be helped.

I take a long walk nearly every day because I love the fresh air. I walk in all seasons but I particularly enjoy the beauty of the red and gold leaves along our Lake Walk in the fall. Sometimes I walk with my husband, Tony, but I often walk alone. While walking I listen to music that inspires me and gives me hope and encouragement.

I use the time to think and to connect with my Higher Power to process my issues whatever they may be. I look at my motives for things. I become aware of my relationships and how each one teaches me something about myself.

It is with joy that I walk with the Master Jesus. He teaches me about how to live joyfully while being in contact with others who are not in the Light. He talks to me about self-respect and about maintaining clear boundaries while daring to love myself in the midst of seeming chaos in the world. He tells me that I'm free to have my own opinions, but that I must allow permission for others to own and express theirs and to see them in the Light without judgment.

He teaches me that I am without sin except in my own mind. He tells me I cannot fail because my goal is to prosper, to love myself, to live free of guilt and judgment of myself and others and to be strong in the Light. My intent is to live joyfully throughout the remaining years of my life until my death.

I am also in joy and gratitude for our divine Mother, Mary, who comes to give counsel when it is needed. We are so blessed to have such divine love and Light available to us.

Honor All That You Are

Honor the part that's in fear,
Talk to it and let it hear,
Your wisdom, your song
Know you're not wrong,
Talk to the part that's in fear.

Honor the part that doubts,
Take its hand in yours as it pouts,
Bring your Light to its side
As it tries to hide,
Honor the part that doubts.

Acknowledge the child inside,
No longer allow it to hide,
Comfort its heart,
Yes, do your part,
Honor the child inside.

Honor the part that grows,
Respect the way that it knows,
Through experience you gain
So honor the pain,
Bless the part that grows.

Honor the Master inside,
In truth you can abide,
Acknowledge what's true
To the inner you,
Honor the Master inside.

There's wisdom in bringing to Light,
All that is of the night,
There are promises, too
From the inner you,
That darkness can turn into Light.

Conscious Living

When life becomes challenging, I know it's time to be grateful. Sometimes it's the seemingly small events like the sun shining, a hot shower, or the smile of a stranger that can bring the Light in.

I have a gratitude list that I have kept over a period of time and add to as I become further aware of things for which I am grateful. I read my list often as it helps to keep my priorities in line by reminding me of what's important in life. My list also keeps me humble and encourages me to continue creating positively both on the spiritual level as well as on earth, for that reason my list comes in very handy and helps keep my problems in perspective. An attitude of gratitude also opens the door for more blessings to come.

I've learned through hard work how to view my challenges as opportunities to learn and to heal my patterns. Therefore, I don't get as upset as I did earlier in my life.

Watching my weight was one of my patterns that I am now healing. If I find myself indulging in judgmental attitudes and controlling behavior regarding my body image or food choices, I get into harmony with my angels and send a message of love and compassion to myself.

Back when I was presenting my workshops, I used to give the participants an exercise that helped to identify the patterns they had chosen to heal. It assisted them in solving their problems by discovering what they were learning through their issues and teaching them how to manifest a greater well-being in their future. I use the exercise myself at times when it feels appropriate.

It is fascinating to me to see how we are so often refining the same character traits such as patience, forgiveness and belief in self, for example, with each issue. In other words we receive throughout various challenges several opportunities to grow in enlightenment.

It is a joy to me to see how the universe works in helping us to find more love and peace in our lives through our experiences. Through repeated patterns we are given countless opportunities to heal without judgment as we progress.

Along with the opportunity to learn and heal, I am grateful that my understanding of life and my self-awareness is growing as is my trust and belief in my Higher Power.

My need for approval and pleasing others is becoming less of an issue as I am trusting more in my own choices and plan for my life. I am indeed grateful to all in the realm of Spirit who benefit me through their love and devotion in helping me to grow and become all I was meant to be.

In counting my blessings I wish to include my husband, Tony, with whom I have experienced much growth, as well as joy. We have had a rich relationship with its ups and downs. Yet through it all we have come out on top. I'm extremely grateful for his sense of humor. I believe there's not a day that goes by that we don't laugh at something. He is my dear friend and I will love him always.

Our daughter Cindy, her husband Lazlo and their children (triplets) Grace, Danny and Benjamen bring us great joy. The children who are now eight-years-old are healthy, lively, intelligent and great fun. We visit them often in Colorado and they come to Duluth in the summer.

I am equally proud of our daughter Leila. We are fortunate having her live near us as she brings light, humor, hope, and healing into our lives.

Also I am fortunate to have very fond memories of my parents who have both passed into spirit. Although they had their own issues and problems, they did their best in providing me with a foundation, which would later benefit me in times of crisis. I feel their presence often and know they are with me with their love and support. I am in gratitude to them for being there now in joy when, for various reasons, they could not always be with me earlier when I was in need. I realize also that it was when I felt most alone in my trials that I gained in spiritual strength and belief in myself.

We often see each other in the astral plane when I go to sleep at night. In the morning upon awakening and when I'm in the Light, I acknowledge them and allow their presence to fill me with peace and gratitude. I am in touch with others in the spirit realm as well who drop by with comforting messages of hope and affirmations that all is indeed well.

I love my sister Dale and her husband Dick. Tony and I enjoy seeing them in Florida when we are there.

I miss my brother Don who is close to my heart. He died after having been ill for some time. He was a bright and gentle soul. His wife Gladys took care of him. I keep her in my thoughts and prayers. She uplifts me with her courage.

I feel privileged as well to have wonderful friends on earth. It is our honor and joy to celebrate birthdays with a group of friends who are part of our past and present. We go back many years and enjoy sharing stories and laughter. I look forward with enthusiasm to our times together. I am indeed fortunate and thankful.

Along with family and friends, I am also grateful to those on earth who provide me with opportunities to grow in Light. I may not like the situations they present me with but with each test I pass I am able to experience more joy in my life.

Truly I am thankful as well that through my trials and the healing of my patterns, I've discovered tools that help me nourish myself. My yoga practice suits me well. I need the flexibility and strength it affords me. In the morning my practice wakes me up while in the evening the relaxing stretches help calm me. On the physical level yoga helps me get in tune with my body while on the spiritual level, it gives me lessons in patience and compassion. I do not expect perfection from myself, which is a good lesson for me. I've learned, as with other things in life, to honor my process and see it in the Light.

Following my yoga practice, I usually spend a short time doing chi gong, which is a gentle form of exercise that combines slow movement, deep breathing and meditation while promoting flexibility and strength. I love the flow of the movements and the feeling of harmony and joy that chi gong gives me. It brings energy to all parts of my body along with many other benefits. Therefore, I'm in gratitude for the added gift of health that comes from this practice.

I have also enjoyed the many health benefits of tai chi at different times in my life having received instruction in several different forms. Again, I love the flow of the movements that feel in harmony with my own energy and leave me with a feeling of well-being and peace.

Music is also a gift to me. For much of the day I enjoy listening to my CDs either in my house or my car. I prefer soft new-age type music that opens my heart and brings me joy. Music can alter my consciousness and raise my vibrations. It has for me the inevitable ability to heal and has always been an important part of my life.

My greatest joy comes from my ability to serve in whatever capacity suits me best. I enjoy sending blessings, prayers and healing for others because I can do that at any time and anywhere. Opening my heart to others helps balance my energy and brings me joy.

I feel privileged to be able to help in this way and it works well for me at this time in my life when we travel a lot. I gain from it also because whatever energy I send out is returned to me. I am glad to be of service as it benefits me as well as those I agree to assist.

As I grow spiritually, I am very cognizant of the various levels of consciousness as well as the existence of a divine plan for myself, and others. Therefore, because of this, there is a tendency to view occurrences with objectivity and to see all "in the Light" as best I can—with purpose and an eventual happy ending either in this world or the life beyond.

This awareness has been a great gift to me and has brought me much comfort and peace when events occur that seem tragic or ill timed.

However, I now understand the importance of allowing myself to feel sadness and grief due to life's "misadventures" whether they happen to me or someone else. I've found it's possible to view events from an objective and spiritual point of view as well as to have the courage to be in my heart and to feel love and compassion for myself, and others.

Learning to live with peace can be challenging especially when one is used to periods of crisis. I needed to learn how to handle stress as well as boredom in new and creative ways rather than falling back into old habits and patterns.

Adapting to a peaceful life requires a conscious commitment to being aware of occasions of worry and the creation of trauma/drama. As I become aware of losing my center, I realize I do have a choice. We all have moments of disappointment and reasons to be upset but we don't have to "live there." I needed to find a new attitude involving faith, trust and a desire to enjoy life, which enables me to stay in the solution.

It's usually the small things that I allow to disturb my peace. The larger life challenges I tend more readily to see in the Light without judgment or fear because I know there is a purpose behind them.

Most things we worry about never happen. I used to go into crisis mode concerning the fear that I did not have my ID card with me when traveling. I always checked to make sure it was in my wallet before leaving home, which it invariably was. Yet on the way to the airport I would panic and have to reassure myself that it was there. Now when the dreaded thought comes to me I simply observe it and let it go.

In my search for peace and joy I found it necessary also to learn to release control and put things in the hands of my Higher Power. I needed to understand that I didn't need all my answers "now" and that it is wise for me to allow things to unfold in God's timing.

When I become preoccupied and bogged down by trivial concerns and worries, I have learned it's beneficial to expand my consciousness by placing my awareness on life outside myself. The release it gives me can be experienced in my body, mind and emotions as it goes from contraction into expansion.

Living in the Light in conscious awareness for me also includes prayer, which is very beneficial to me. Along with thanking God for my blessings and divine protection, I like to take the time to pray for others. It gets me out of myself and that which I send out comes back to me and assists me with my own issues. I have learned that it's important that I see those I pray for in a positive way. They need to be viewed as whole and in the Light.

It also helps to ask for clarity and "knowingness" concerning whatever current problems or conditions I may have. Further, it benefits me to ask to be prepared on all levels for opportunities that come my way and to be made aware of and respond to my challenges in divine Light.

Lastly, it's helpful to ask that I use my energy each day for the highest good. That way my choices are of the greatest benefit to me as well as others.

My experiences with my Higher Power are truly wondrous and leave me with a greater faith and trust in God as well as in myself.

Living in the Light also implies staying in the solution with whatever comes my way. One day as I was driving back from Grand Marais, Minnesota, while listening to beautiful music on a favorite CD, I had the opportunity to experience a lesson on attitude adjustment. The spring day was gorgeous, sunny, without a cloud in the sky. The single-lane highway upon which I was traveling is well known for its spectacular scenery. Incidentally, this was one of the main reasons I chose to make the trip—to enjoy the ride and the beauty.

Along the way I had to stop to deliver some fliers. When I got back onto the main road I found myself behind a huge semi that totally blocked my view. Needless to say, I was quite upset as I knew that the truck would be in front of me for many miles if not all the way home. Passing would be difficult and dangerous as there were many cars ahead of it. So I decided to stay where I was and put up with the stress of having several cars behind me as well as the monstrous truck ahead of me.

However, as my irritation grew, I thought, perhaps there's a lesson for me here. My thoughts turned to the driver of the truck. I said to myself, "This man is earning a living. He has as much right to being here as I do and he's probably a nice guy." I began thinking more kindly toward him as our little line of cars sped forward single file down the highway. I sent positive thoughts as well to the drivers behind me. This seemed to alleviate the stress I was feeling, driving for so long in this "caravan." The truck remained ahead of me for many miles and eventually turned off.

Then to my great surprise, I discovered I actually missed it! Changing my attitude and behavior helped me to open my heart that had closed down due to my being upset. Mentally I thanked the truck driver for the lesson and for helping me to feel good again.

Since that experience I've become even more aware of how one can sense the feelings of other drivers nearby. I really believe irritation and anger directed at someone even silently can be upsetting enough to cause an accident. I'm very conscious now as to how I use my energy and thoughts on the highway.

For me, it's extremely beneficial to laugh. Laughter helps me to keep my life in perspective and prevents me from taking myself too seriously. I once had the enlightening experience of getting on the wrong plane en route home from Denver. I had been on the phone with a friend and was listening to music on my headphones when I heard the numbers of what I thought was my flight being called. I passed through several airport personnel who each looked at my ticket. Once we were airborne, someone asked over the speaker if Jill Downs was on board. I raised my hand. The airline hostess asked where I was headed. I told her, "Duluth." She said, "Well, we're going to International Falls." They alerted my husband at the Duluth airport who was waiting for me and, of course, he got a huge laugh out of it.

Meanwhile, I had to fly back down to Minneapolis and start over with nothing to do or read because my carry-on bag had to be stowed with the luggage. Needless to say, what started out as a delightful quick trip from Denver turned out to be excruciatingly long.

I was quite sensitive about this and being president of the church board at the time wasn't thrilled about people knowing about my mishap. I felt a bit ridiculous and stupid.

This indeed was a lesson in not taking myself so seriously. There was a part of me that actually thought this episode was hilarious as did others who knew me. I needed to let go of my bruised ego, which in time, I did.

Honoring my own processes through understanding that I'm in healing with my various issues and not expecting perfection from myself enables me to stay on the solution. I can put Light on situations that confuse me releasing them to my Higher Power knowing the answers will come in God's time. I can also be aware of and avoid negativity that comes from many sources and view love as the bottom line, beginning with love of myself and expanding out to others.

In learning to live in conscious awareness I've been grateful for the understanding of the concept that we are all ONE—meaning that, what we do for others will be done for us. When I wish health, success and joy for another, I'm sending it also to me. When I am kind and compassionate towards myself, I'm able and willing to open my heart to others.

I'm grateful as well for the opportunity to learn my lessons, to find new solutions that are positive, healthy and empowering, to take every doubt, fear or pattern to my highest desire, and to see it as truth, and to explore the magic of life where maybe I was once asleep. Thankfully, now I am awake and in joy and freedom.

Seek for Fulfillment

Release your doubt,
Release your fear.
Enjoy the earth
While you are here.

Follow your heart
And follow your dreams,
You may be surprised—
Life's not what it seems.

For the way is prepared
When you follow your Light,
As angels go first,
To make your path bright.

And be not discouraged
When you make a mistake,
For experience is gathered
On each road we take.

And who is to say
If one has erred?
Do not be afraid,
Do not be scared.

Perhaps your adventure
Was needed, you see,
To help with your goal
To be all you can be.

So, judge not your past
And live for today.
Take in each moment
And go on your way.

Look for your essence,
For that which is you.
Seek for your spirit
In all that you do.

This brings you to balance,
To that even place...
This brings you to peace,
To that sacred space

From where we make choices,
That keep us on course,
And opens our hearts
In love, to the Source.

Nature and Healing

I believe a whole new world opens up as we open our hearts, minds and spirits to the divine aspects of nature. I am in awe for example, as I sense the spirits of the flowers, plants and trees.

Tony has a gift for growing flowers. His large planter is filled with a colorful fusion along with a window box of gorgeous begonias that are large, brightly colored and look as though they are made of tissue paper. September is my favorite time for the flowers due to the way the early fall Light brings out their vivid hues.

One day when I was in our kitchen, I became aware of a gorgeous red rose that Tony had picked from his garden and put in a vase on our counter. The rose spoke to me through my intuition. It felt both startling and very natural at the same time! It said, "Look at me." That was all it took to release whatever concerns I had at the time. I felt overwhelmed with gratitude and was indeed transformed both by the message and the beauty of the flower.

On another occasion I was looking for a flowering plant to serve as a centerpiece for a party for Cindy, Laszlo and the triplets who were coming from Colorado. I walked into a grocery store and was immediately faced with dozens of plants and flowers of all kinds. One particular plant with brightly colored pink flowers again spoke to my heart through its energy telling me it was the plant I was to take home for my party. This was not the kind of plant I was initially looking for but after it communicated with me, I knew this was the one to choose. I was overjoyed. The rest is history. This same plant has been with us bringing us hope and joy as it continues to bless us year after year.

Many years ago when we lived in our former residence, I can remember sitting in an armchair facing the window that looked out into the front yard. There was a large tree whose branches were moving and bending toward me in the wind against a cloudy late afternoon sky. It was a dark and dreary day. I can remember feeling rather blue at the time. It seemed perfectly natural to be listening through my heart as the spirit of the tree brought me kind thoughts of wisdom and truth.

At the time I most likely thought it was my imagination. In fact, I didn't think much about it at all. However, now years later, having had many more experiences communicating with the natural world, I recognize the authenticity of the event. Our Creator has magnificent and boundless ways of getting our attention.

On another occasion I was participating in a Tai Chi class at a New Age store near our home. I'd been coming there for weeks and yet had never noticed a large amethyst that sat on the floor near where we practiced. One day it got my attention. It said that I was to buy it and take it home. It belonged to me. I've heard people say this about things they want but I had never had such an experience come with such clarity and, yes I bought it the next day. It has sat by our fireplace and shared its lovely energy with us for many years.

Another time I saw a lovely amethyst that I really liked and wondered if it would possibly be mine. When I tuned into it, I got a "No." This was to go to somebody else. I find it so fascinating how some expressions of energy are meant for us and others are not. God is indeed in charge.

For years I've been interested in stones and crystals for the energy they hold. I have a dish of colored stones on our coffee table. They include rose quartz, aventurine and amethyst. Rose quartz is my favorite. It holds the energy of love and compassion. I've also always been drawn to the amethyst, which I believe facilitates spiritual transformation and empowerment.

On one occasion I bought a necklace in Maui. At that time I was practicing psychometry—the art of feeling or sensing the energy of stones and other objects. Almost immediately I had a vision like a photograph of an aristocratic Hawaiian family. It was a joy to me to connect with the energy. It felt like there was a purpose to my buying the piece of jewelry and that it was a gift from the woman who had owned and worn the necklace.

One of the many ways nature affects us is through the weather. A sunny day can surely make me smile while a gray day often challenges me to remain in the Light. One day in late winter while I was taking a walk, I became aware of the possible symbolism in nature with regard to what I needed to heal in my life.

The day was overcast—the clouds dark and ominous suggestive of the slight twinge of fear of the unknown I was feeling. The wind was strong, signaling changing conditions in my life for which I knew not whether to be grateful. The sidewalk was icy warning of the need to be cautious as well as patient. This was about the "long haul" and the need for compassion for myself as well as faith and trust in tomorrow. Suddenly, I saw a bird that appeared to enjoy getting my attention. I understood his message and I responded by releasing my fear and dread of the future and opening my heart to hope and eagerness for a new adventure.

In my experience symbolism extends itself to the animal kingdom as well. I love the animals and believe in what they have to teach us. They come at different times of the year marking the seasons as well as the hours of the day. This is to me part of what the magic is all about. I feel so honored with each encounter I have in the physical reality, and have been blessed by their spirits as well. I am delighted when I am at peace to tune into the messages they bring me, as it's always something I need at the time. When we moved into our home in 1995, we were amazed at the amount of wildlife that surrounded us. Our mailman said to me one day, "You have more animals here than they have at the zoo." It seemed strange too, because we live in the city just off a busy street tucked in on the shore of Lake Superior. It wasn't long after we moved in that we began enjoying visits from a wide variety of animals and birds.

One night we looked out our living room window and saw two large black bears. They were engaging in playful combat batting each other around as they made powerful huffing and grunting sounds. The sight was awesome. I felt privileged to witness what appeared to be such a private encounter. The insight to be gained was about being more playful in my own life. The bear is special to me. He reminds me of my inner strength and that it's time to go within and process my emotions, which brings renewal. The bear teaches self-reliance and encourages me to be in confidence in my decisions. I have had numerous magical encounters with bears. One night I happened to wake up and while walking into the kitchen, I saw the shadow of a large bear behind our closed curtain in the living room. He was walking the length of our deck. The bear sighting took less than a minute. I was enthralled. The synchronicity of the event amazed me. I know my Higher Power awakened me to see the animal lumbering by the window. It was a time in my life when I was processing a great deal. The bear reminded me that I was exactly where I needed to be in my life.

The deer come in our yard almost every day. Often they will look right at us even though they are several yards from the house. When I am quiet and at peace I'm able to tune into the messages they bring. One day as I was driving on a city street, I had to stop as ten deer crossed in front of my car. Some believe that the number ten represents completion. In any case, it felt significant to me and I was encouraged by the encounter. I believe the deer are about compassion and gentleness. One summer we had two sets of twin fawns appear with their mothers. My sense is their message has to do with forgiveness—a theme that cycles periodically and commands my attention. The softness and sweetness of the little fawns helped me to open my heart in love and forgiveness for myself, and others.

I had to get past the common thought that the raccoon is merely a mischievous animal that can be as destructive as it is courageous. We are often visited by families of raccoons and though I would remind myself how ferocious they could be, I couldn't help but love these masked "bandits." One summer we left a large bag of dry dog food next to the door on our porch. We had been feeding the foxes that came in the yard. One night we left the window open and a raccoon had gnawed through the screen and entered the sun porch and chewed through the bag of dry dog food and then left the same way he came in. We were very lucky no more damage was done.

At another time when we lived in our old house, we had two wonderful cats that we acquired through a friend. One evening as Tony was in the kitchen, he noticed an animal eating out of the cat dish. He thought, as he saw the animal out of the corner of his eye, that Eddie (our beloved cat) seemed to have gotten fatter. He then noticed it was indeed a raccoon that had walked in the open door from our deck, waddled through the dining room and into the kitchen where he was enjoying a meal of cat food. He then, when finished, ambled out back through the dining room and out the deck door. I was told by my friends in spirit that the raccoon wanted to "play and to eat."

These stories bring me hope and fond memories of sharing space with our raccoon friends as well as gratitude for the protection of our home.

On occasion we're apt to see a skunk in our yard, usually near our deck in the evenings. However, one day as I was heading up the driveway, a skunk crossed right in front of my car seemingly in full control of the situation, which he was. I stopped my car and let him pass. The day after, in the middle of the afternoon, the skunk crossed our lawn in the back of our house by the lake. It was then that I realized because the animal made itself so visible and obvious to me there was a message from him. The skunk brings me knowledge of myself in relation to others telling me to honor myself and to be in confidence in my decisions. Skunk reminds me to respect myself and my life choices, while seeing myself in Light and truth. Tony saw the skunk cross the yard and got a closer look. She had a baby skunk she was carrying in her mouth, a catalyst for us regarding tenderness. The skunk is a wonderful teacher.

Years ago I was confronted with a situation in which others were being dishonest with me. I happened to notice a weasel walk right up our front walk and look into the window to the right of the door. I was astounded and overjoyed because I knew this encounter had special significance for me. I was too emotional at the time to obtain my own information as to the symbology of the weasel so I relied on Ted Andrews' book *Animal Speak*. He associated the weasel, among other things, as a warning that there was deception around you if a weasel showed up in your life. This was indeed the case and the affirmation surely enriched my life.

We are very fortunate to have eagles crossing our path. My angels once said to me, "An eagle soaring is our attempt to reach you from the spirit world. It is a promise of success in your endeavors." The eagle from my view symbolizes upliftment, spiritual growth, and trust in the future.

One day I was in awe as I witnessed two eagles flying in circles as though in a dance resembling a figure eight. When I asked if there was a message to be gained, I heard it symbolized, "harmony and peace and the notion that all's right with the world and my place in it." I was indeed grateful and humbled by the affirmation.

On another occasion as I was learning to trust the messages of the natural world, I had the spirit of an eagle visit me when I was in my Pilates class. I was both surprised and thankful. The purpose was to reaffirm my trust in my process.

We have a friend who passed away several years ago. He had been very much of an outdoorsman and had told me one day that the eagle was a special power animal for him. My friend visited me from spirit as he does fairly often and told me that the next time I saw an eagle he would be there. I did view the eagle majestically soaring off to my right as I drove down a busy thoroughfare—a rather unlikely place to see and eagle, I thought.

Nature's gifts never cease to amaze me. One day several years ago, I was looking out the window on our sun porch and saw what appeared to be a large gray rag draped over a statue we have just outside our deck door. I looked again and saw it was a very large great gray owl. It looked straight at me. I prayed it would stay there while I called Tony. As soon as we both got a good look at it, it flew away.

The owl brings to my mind past lives, particularly a Native American lifetime. It has an aura that is at once both magical and haunting. Rather than connecting the owl to darkness, I prefer to associate it with spiritual growth, death, rebirth and empowerment. We were stunned at its presence and honored to be so gifted with its role in our lives.

The crow is another bird that deserves mention. They remind me to listen. Their squawking encourages me to "be present and alert to all that is around me—both visible and invisible." They teach patience and once again I am reminded to see them in the Light.

While the crow is haunting and mystical in spirit and appearance with the shiny blue-black color, the hummingbird to me brings joy and playfulness. When I become too serious, the hummingbird comes to brighten my day.

Butterflies I've found have similar energy. Whenever I have butterflies dance around me as they do occasionally on my walks, I'm reminded to be joyful and carefree in my life. They tell me all is well in my world and that there is peace and forgiveness for myself, and others.

I've had two experiences with spiders that have enabled me to heal some issues and bring others into awareness. I've always been afraid of spiders. One day I encountered a spider in our home. I looked at it and it spooked me because I felt a message coming from the spider saying, "Don't be afraid of me." Since that time I've looked at spiders differently. Their message to me when they appear, I believe, is a reminder to think creatively or to engage in some creative endeavor.

I'm still a bit squeamish at times where spiders are concerned, especially following an experience I had in Maui. One year I encountered a very large cane spider in our condo. It was at night. I'd been lying on the couch in the living room. The spider walked toward me, stopped and looked at me. Humbled, as well as terrified, I got the insect spray and killed it. As this all was going on there was another higher part of me that felt much guilt and incredible sadness, as I knew the spider was my teacher. To forgive myself and love myself through the experience was my challenge. I am in awe of how nature comes through with its lessons.

From our condo in Maui we are fortunate to be able to see much whale activity in the ocean. The whales are said to be the guardians of the sea. Their sound sends shivers up my spine and is reminiscent of the creative life force. A whale under the sea brings to my mind divine Light and latent or potential power while one that is breaching reminds me to release any fears, believe in myself, and become all I was meant to be in this life.

While on a whale-watch excursion one day, our daughter, Cindy, and her husband, Laszlo, and I were blessed by being surrounded by several whales that were swimming all around as well as underneath our boat. It was awesome as well as a bit frightening although I had the sense that I was in the presence of high vibrational energy. I get goose bumps as I write about this magnificent mammal. Whenever I see the whale, I know I'm in the presence of divine Light, love, and protection.

Once while at the zoo, I was observing a turtle in a large tank. I became aware through my intuition that he was communicating with me. He told me that he responds positively to the Light and kindness of others. He said he wishes to be treated with respect. As I remember, he was very old. He also gave me some information on my own life for which I was both stunned and grateful.

In Florida where we often visit, we stay in a condo that overlooks a pond. There is a small "raft" on the pond where the turtles came to rest and sit in the sun. Often we see ten turtles on the raft—once again possibly signifying the idea of completion.

The turtle reminds me to stay grounded and connected to the earth. He also reminds me to slow down and have patience and belief in myself as well as trust in tomorrow. To be content with "the long haul" is included in the message to me from the animal.

One day while on our walk, Tony and I encountered a turtle that had obviously been hit by a car as it was attempting to cross the street. It sat on the edge of the sidewalk sheltered by the foliage. His shell was broken and he was gravely wounded. Our intuition told us not to feed it or move it. In my mind I called on Jesus who wrapped him in love and protection that allowed him to go to sleep while his spirit was then released. I felt grateful that we were able to help the turtle die in peace.

One day as I looked out on the pond from our deck, I saw an alligator sunning himself on the "turtle raft." Needless to say the birds and turtles that had been enjoying the day there quickly dispersed to make way for the new visitor. No one fools with the alligator.

On another occasion I "ran into" an alligator on my walk to a pond near our condo. He was in the water half submerged in the middle of the pond. He was easy to spot and seemed definitely "in charge." I heard my angels say that he brings peace to you. He trusts you. It's important not to go into fear with the alligator or any wild animals but regard them in the Light.

Years ago we had two cats named Eddie and Gray Kitty who brought great joy to our family. They both lived to an old age and gave us many gifts. Their personalities were different but each just as lovable in their own way.

Eddie didn't appear to be as smart as Gray Kitty but was a wonderful healer as he would snuggle next to you and bring comfort and healing to whatever was troubling you. Eddie could often be found in the morning sitting at the bottom of the stairs crying until one of us opened our bedroom door. He would then rush in, hop up on the bed and purr loudly until we'd fall back to sleep.

Eddie enjoyed the outdoors. However, one day Gray Kitty, who was a gorgeous Russian Blue cat and was very classy (he looked like he ought to be wearing a tuxedo), was in a stand-off with his nemesis, Toby. Toby was the black and white cat from next door. Eddie was looking out the window watching. Suddenly he wanted to join the fray. So we opened the door and Eddie ran out onto the deck attacking Gray Kitty instead of Toby. In all the excitement he became a bit confused. Not all of us are meant to be warriors.

One day an aging Eddie was brought to our good friend the vet, who called us telling us it was best if we let Eddie go. It was time. Later on I was sitting in my chair meditating and I actually felt the needle go in my arm. Eddie was, at that time, being allowed to die. I sent him love and Light and knew he was not alone. Later that evening I had a meditation class I was responsible for at the church. During our period of silence I felt Eddie's spirit happily jump into my lap. I was thrilled!

Since the death of our cats I very often hear that one or both of them are with me for a visit. I believe they come when they are needed to soothe, calm, and to also give hope that we will indeed see our animal friends again upon our own death and reawakening in the spirit world.

Participating with nature is a joy to me. Depending on where we are at any given time, we are blessed with the wonder and magic of the natural world. Often I conspire with the universe asking that Tony and I be made aware of the wildlife around us so long as we are not harmed. This seems to bring us encounters with animals and birds we may not otherwise have been fortunate enough to experience.

Nature often brings enlightenment, reassurance and great joy. Tuning into the beauty of nature often brings me into my heart as it releases the worries and concerns of the day. It teaches me to listen and be alert to what may be hiding in the forest or flying overhead and how that reverberates in my soul. Even just a short walk in the evening settles my spirit as I open to the natural energy around me while a full moon on the lake reminds me that I am alive and participating in life.

Following my Kundalini opening and always with the guidance and assistance of the Master Jesus and my guides and angels, I felt honored and privileged to explore alternate realities that included other kingdoms, other intelligences, other beings, other worlds and universes. I was made aware of other levels of being—the unconscious, conscious and superconscious and experienced time travel as well as our alignment with the stars and planets including Jupiter, the Pleiades, Mars, Uranus, and Saturn.

Further, I greatly enjoyed experiencing the peace and joy of the angelic kingdom including visits from the archangels, the wonder of the fairy kingdom, the elementals as well as divine light-beings who help ease the pain and suffering through raising the consciousness of mankind. I was also gratified and illuminated by the teachings of the masters who continue to bless me with their wisdom. I was able to explore other spiritual realms of consciousness including universal consciousness, the lower, middle and upper astral planes including the place where many of us go when we die and return to Spirit. Further I was also honored to glimpse the Akashic Records that hold the stored history of each individual life, and of course, there is the God consciousness or All That Is. I discovered that we seek knowledge from other realms and realities in order to gain information concerning ourselves and our relationship to them, to the Universe and to God.

Where we are in our consciousness affects how we see other realms and levels of reality. We are watched over by hosts of angels, but do we see them? Do we see the fairy under a bush or the elemental in charge of seeing that our car runs smoothly?

I gained knowledge of how other kingdoms influence our perception of reality. In other words, this explains how we are affected by the astral realm with thoughts bombarding and mixing with our own. I was made aware of how hosts of angels affect weather patterns and storms, earthquakes and tidal waves. It is fascinating as well how we see other beings through our own filters—our own perception of the way things are and how the nature of reality changes as we grow.

Our perception changes as we move closer to spirit and live according to the Universal Laws—Spiritual Law. As we live in harmony with ourselves and mankind, we become more sensitive to spirit and thus are able to enjoy a greater potential in opening up to other realms. In this way we may become more fulfilled and are able to more fully realize our potential as human beings as we are able to see our relationship to the whole and in doing so make the world a better place.

It is fascinating to see how different realms and levels of reality relate to each other and have the potential to help us to grow and change our patterns. For example, the Hierarchy, a body of Light-Beings, helps us adjust to a new vibrational level as the earth is being raised to a higher frequency requiring us to change our attitudes and beliefs about ourselves and our world. As we release our fears and grow in love, we are helping raise the consciousness of all mankind.

It was a relief for me to discover I had a unique opportunity to share my journey with others. Having these experiences was part of my chosen path. I do not go into details of "travels" because they occurred years ago and are difficult to put into words but will remain forever in my heart.

I shall always be grateful to have had a mentor and good friend in the spirit world who was extremely humorous and had me actually laughing out loud when my experiences became too intense and challenging for me. I have learned that it's laughter and joy that help propel us to new heights and a closer relationship to God and it's often the natural world that helps bring healing to our bodies, mind and emotions.

Count Your Blessings

Be grateful for your blessings,
For all that's come to you.
Be grateful for the gifts
That God has brought to you.

Be grateful for your talents.
Discover what they are.
Develop your abilities
And know you will go far.

Create what you desire;
Know what you like to do;
Follow your heart;
Keep your vision true to you.

Don't take your life for granted,
Be grateful, do your part
For the seed of health is planted
Right within your heart.

Be grateful for your friends
And for your family, too.
Give thanks for their lives
And their relationship to you.

Be grateful for your past
And the lessons you've endured.
Give thanks for the experience
And wisdom you've secured.

Be grateful for the pain
That does come your way,
'Cause hidden in each hurt
Lies a gift that's here to stay.

Give thanks for all the help
You've obtained throughout the years.
Be grateful to the angels
Who come to dry your tears.

Be grateful for the knowledge
That they do impart,
And for the gift of healing
As they impress your heart.

Give gratitude to nature
And all it has to give.
Be grateful to the animals
And all with whom you live.

Give thanks for the flowers
That one day will be gone,
And for the plants and trees
That tell us we belong.

For as we live together
In nature we confide,
And we may strike a balance
With all that is inside.

Give thanks for our choices,
Our ability to choose,
And for all the different voices
There's a thought we shouldn't lose.

It's a special attitude
That we must hold so dear.
It's an attitude of gratitude
Sustained throughout the year.

Healthy Lifestyle

I was never grossly overweight but have suffered with body image issues on and off much of my life. My mother was constantly dieting so I heard about weight loss all her life. Counting calories was the big thing back then.

My family was, for the most part, into pretty healthy eating. As children, we were always told to "clean our plates." I remember being left in the dining room alone to finish my dinner. I used to call the dog in and I'd give Vicki, our Airedale, my dinner under the table. I can also remember lining my peas up under my knife hoping they wouldn't be detected.

I believe all this, coupled with the trend to be thin as seen in magazines and on TV, helped contribute to my concerns about food and weight—me and thousands of others.

Throughout my life I have continued struggling with my body image. I was even weighing myself in the middle of the night if I happened to wake up. If my weight started to go up, I would panic. Sometimes I thought that by monitoring myself either on the scale or in the mirror, I would somehow be able to "control" my weight and get it down to where I wanted it. In actuality the more I watched the scale and my body, the "bigger" I became, thus reinforcing the self-fulfilling prophecy.

When I understood it was all about loving myself, I stopped monitoring. I gave up the scale and told myself I was just fine as I was. It was at that point things began to change for me. I also began to visualize being healthy and happy. I've worked with visualization and manifestation for years and discussed both processes in my workshops as well and find the skills work in every area of my life. Loving and accepting myself as I am still takes practice. I'm by no means perfect but I am grateful to have understood the lesson and given up attempting to control my weight.

My spirit guides and angels often talk to me about the importance of eating "in the Light." I've found that I serve myself best when I follow my heart and eat in love and peace. Generally, I consider myself a pretty healthy eater. Yet, when we travel and stop at the Minneapolis Airport, I most often always have a McDonald's egg and sausage

McMuffin. I don't judge it or feel guilty about it. I just enjoy it. It's the judgment I bring to food and eating that I feel is harmful to me. If I choose to eat something that is not considered to be "healthy," it's important that I not feel guilty about it, but savor it instead.

If I feel something is bad for me, most likely it will be. If I feel something is going to make me fat, it will. In contrast eating a piece of cake in the Light and following my heart can serve me well. Worrying about food and eating for me is unhealthy and takes the joy out of living. I believe I can eat very healthy food, but if my heart and attitude are not in the Light and if I'm not enjoying it, my efforts will be wasted.

I think it's the same with vitamins and other supplements. I used to take them no matter what. My guidance since has been to rely more on my intuition. Since then, when we travel even for several weeks, I give them a rest and don't take them at all. I may then upon my return home reintroduce them gradually according to what feels right to me.

My angels also tell me that it is also necessary to take supplements in the Light. Visualizing the desired outcome from ingesting anything is very helpful. What do I want to gain from taking this supplement? I need to view prescriptions in the same way. If I'm about to take something, I'll sometimes hear my guidance tell me, "You are not in the Light on it," meaning I have doubts about what I'm taking or I'm not focusing on my intention with it.

When I feel like eating a couple of cookies or a piece of cake, I try not to judge it but go directly to my heart and ask if that's what I really want. Sometimes it is and I eat the desired food in freedom and in joy. At other times I know I'm being dishonest with myself and using my creative mind, I can transform the energy and choose instead something healthier and more to my liking. I'm learning to accept responsibility for my choices.

I believe we are all different and that which works for one may not work for all. I also believe time is a big factor regarding healing our bodies and weight issues. I did lots of reading, as I know many people do, on health, nutrition, and various diets. I now know I have to do what feels right for me.

My goal has been to heal the issues surrounding my beliefs about food, weight loss, and body image. Subscribing to another's point of view on how I should eat no longer works for me, as I need to learn to trust myself. There are certain attitudes, beliefs and practices I've begun to subscribe to since embarking on my healing process.

Mentally I ask God to bless my food. This puts divine Light into what I eat which gives me greater energy, health, and balance as I also ask to be of service to others. It's also important to be in the Light myself as I eat. Being mindful and eating slowly is another good practice. I have had a tendency to gulp my food down—a habit that I developed in childhood. Eating slowly and deliberately takes practice but I know it is much better for my digestion and overall health. Also, in order that I don't eat too much, I have a signal in my mind that informs me when my body has been nourished. This is where trusting myself comes in. I believe we all know much more about this subject than we think we do. I have an expression I say to myself at certain times where trust in my own being is needed that says, "You do too know." The goal is to listen to my inner voice. There are times however, when I choose not to heed my intuition and continue to eat, but I'm very aware of what I'm doing and choose not to judge myself, but to stay in the Light. I'm happiest when I follow my heart because it brings me joy and health.

As far as what to eat, I follow my intuition. Once more, "You do to know," comes in handy. I really do know what is good for me and what will bring me joy. I also know if I'm honest with myself when I'm eating for emotional reasons. Sometimes it's really water I want. Other times I recognize that I need to nourish myself in another way.

I don't subscribe to being rigid about food. Eating in the Light—that is, eating in peace and joy is what I've come to understand is what is important and beneficial. A pizza can be just as good for me as a salad, depending on my belief about it and if I'm in the Light on it.

Being in Light and joy I found out is also important regarding exercise. When I was young, I partook in lots of sports including skiing, swimming, tennis and waterskiing. I was active and loved the activities I indulged in. Therefore, being happy with what I was doing was not an issue. I naturally enjoyed these sports. Later on I took up jogging and discovered the joy of the natural high.

It was when I joined classes to lose weight that I stopped enjoying physical activity to the extent that I used to. As I began obsessing about losing those ten pounds that I started to feel as though I was a rat in a maze or a cat chasing its tail. My goal became more and more elusive.

I had lost the joy of exercise for its own sake and became exasperated about not seeing the results I wanted on my body. I was focused more on health and weight loss and not on enjoyment of the activities.

One day as I was taking a walk, I became concerned because I feared that I wasn't walking fast enough to get a good cardio workout. I heard Tom (a wonderful Light-Being I had called on to help me with exercise) say to me, "I would rather see you walk at a comfortable pace and enjoy watching the birds or a chipmunk climb a tree. Enjoying your walk and surroundings and having a good time is as important if not more important than focusing on getting your heart rate up. Love is more important than anything for your heart and physiological processes. Love heals. Enjoy the sunshine and nature and you will benefit greatly."

I'm not against doing exercise specifically designed to help one's health but I now believe in keeping it in perspective. The worst thing I could do would be to do an exercise I didn't like just to lose weight.

At any rate, I believe in the importance of staying active. My mother used to be a wonderful tennis player when she was in her 30s. Then she got rheumatoid arthritis, which curtailed her activities to a great extent. She could no longer play tennis, garden or do other things she so enjoyed. I've been so grateful for my health. My intent is to stay healthy and active for as long as I can.

I enjoy lots of activities and sports. For me, variety is important both for health and enjoyment. I love to swim, walk, ski, do yoga, tai chi and chi gung. I also enjoy golf with a friend and because I'm a beginner, I have the opportunity to laugh at my ineptness. Keeping a sense of humor makes it all worthwhile. Once again, being in the Light makes the difference whether or not I enjoy and benefit from a particular activity. I enjoy some activities alone and it's generally brought to my attention whether I'm benefiting from a particular activity or not. I'll think to myself, "it's time for a walk," and sometimes I become aware that a walk isn't really what I want right now. On occasion I find I'm doing an activity because I think I should, not because I want to. I can, however, with my awareness, change my attitude, which will then make the activity a positive experience. I like to call on extra help and energy from God for help with sports and other physical activities.

I find through my intuition that I get instruction as well as love and encouragement. When I had returned to downhill skiing after a long lapse, I had the privilege of enjoying a teacher from Spirit who was strong in the Light and who made my experience with skiing an adventure to remember. Although I never thought of myself as an expert at skiing, I went on to teach the sport and I believe it was this being who gave me encouragement after not having skied for a long time.

I also call on Jesus, the angels and archangels to assist me in all my endeavors including my issues with health—whether it be physical, mental, emotional, or spiritual—while through my heightened awareness I continue to gain from my experiences. Several years ago I participated in Jazzercise classes and later a Pilates class. Exercising wasn't new to me but I'd wanted to drop a few pounds and so was focused on the scale and my body image. Finding that I wasn't getting the results I wanted, although I highly recommend both forms of exercise, I joined a workout center and was grateful to get into the hands of a wonderful personal trainer. We became friends and I had an enjoyable time there.

However, my intuition told me that my goal on a soul level wasn't just about getting trim and losing weight. It was about self-love. Learning self-acceptance and to have compassion for myself was more important and had to come first. Once I became enlightened in my process, the healing would begin. I began to view myself with love and stopped comparing myself to others. I understood my choice and learned to have patience with myself, knowing I had all the time in the world to heal. Eventually I left my friends and trainer, choosing instead to go to the workout center near our home. This was mostly due to my schedule change. As a result, I am working out alone using the skills I learned from my trainer and others. It works well for me and I greatly enjoy it. I also returned to Jazzercise. Changing my routine, being creative, trying new things, and, above all, relaxing about it, makes exercise fun and beneficial to me

I have found that when I'm in an emotional crisis many of my intentions for living a healthy lifestyle can go down the drain. It's important that I don't judge myself and that I have compassion for myself, and others. It also helps me to pray for those who are in similar circumstances even if I don't know who they are. A general prayer sent out to the universe to help those in need helps to get me out of myself and balance my energy.

Also because, during an emotional crisis, I have a tendency to let go of certain practices that I ordinarily do each day. Therefore, I created a list of important things I want to remember to do each day in order to keep me in health and balance. Examples might include drinking water, exercise, reading my gratitude list, meditation, yoga, taking my supplements, visualization, releasing judgments of myself and others, and journaling. My list changes periodically and includes practices that I feel are particularly important at the time. Each day I check things off. This is not for judgment, but to alert myself as to what I need to attend to. I do not use my list all the time, but occasionally find it helpful, particularly during a stressful time or when it feels important to get back on track. I've found that when I am able to stay strong in the Light through my challenges, I remain God-centered so that my list isn't necessary as I am, "in the flow," and the needed guidance is there for me.

My intent now is to respect myself and to honor my process in releasing old issues and patterns involving my body, weight, nutrition, and exercise. My goal is to love and accept myself the way I am at any given moment. For a long time I was fearful and unhappy with my habit of night eating, but now I accept it as part of my process. I do not attempt to eliminate it, but honor its place in my life.

I do not diet, count points or calories, but learn to trust myself regarding my food choices. There are no good or bad foods, only choices to be made in my heart. I do not judge myself if I gain weight but see it all as part of my process and forgive myself for my "mistakes." I am in the process of releasing my struggle with the issue. I eat without guilt or feeling badly about what I'm consuming. My goal involves comparing myself to no one and to lighten way up on the issue, releasing all that doesn't bring me joy.

Accepting our Bodies

Accepting our bodies
Without a fuss
Is challenging
For most of us.

As we stare
At imperfections
We loudly voice
Our strong objections.

Yet if it's peace you want instead
Change the image in your head.
See yourself how you want to be
Visualization is the key.

And when you find you want to whine,
See yourself as looking fine.
Instead of going in to a snit,
See yourself as looking fit.

Affirm your health and energy, too.
This tells your body what to do.
It will conform to your commands,
Yet diligence this plan demands.

And when you want to shed a tear,
Talk to the image in the mirror.
Affirm your strength, affirm your health,
Have compassion for yourself.

Fat or thin, short or tall,
Whether we are large or small
Doesn't matter in the end.
It's our soul we must attend.

Inner beauty is the key.
Your Light is what others see.
That which shines from your eyes,
Your soul tells all, and it is wise.

Transformation and Empowerment

Years ago when our good friend invited us to go to the Bahamas, we went without hesitation. The trip meant fun and freedom from responsibility for me with two young children at home. I gladly partook in the alcohol that was readily available and all in all enjoyed myself immensely, though there was a part of me that felt with some guilt that my goals of escape and partying were not in my best interest. I didn't understand that that time in my life was significant and not without purpose.

As I look back on that trip, I've learned not to judge myself so harshly as I sometimes did. We were choosing a fun time, and though we were drinking, for the most part, we were in the Light!

A similar situation arose in regard to smoking cigarettes. I chose to stop smoking about a year or so after I went into treatment in 1980. I later began smoking again following my Kundalini experience. I remember at that time that my angels told me very clearly not to judge my cigarette habit. They told me I would let go of it in time and to be kind and gentle with myself. I was so grateful that I was able to lighten up on myself and because of this, it was much easier when the time came, to release the habit.

I'm aware that when I judge myself for anything, the pattern tends to repeat itself until I've learned to release judgment and forgive whatever thought or behavior in which I'm engaging. To view myself in the Light and send love and healing to my process assists me as well.

I often hear my angels tell me to laugh at my compulsions and idiosyncrasies. It's helpful to know that I can grow out of "bad" habits. Also I prefer to make healthier choices because I want to, not because I have to. I prefer healing in the Light. It works best for me if I ask for divine help, trust in my intuition and my process and release judgment.

Feeling unworthy or not good enough is familiar to many of us. We see others as much better than we are—more intelligent, talented, better looking, etc. We are, indeed, all unique and in varying stages of growth and understanding regarding the issues we face every day. We all have plans for our lives that vary in accordance with whatever we've chosen to learn in this lifetime. We all come from our core beliefs and values.

We land on the moon, we play the piano, we run with the bulls, and we're great knitters. Solitude is for some, while others are rock stars.

We all have goals whether we understand them or not. We each have reasons for being on this earth while we all play roles and function at different levels. As we see others in the Light, we, in turn, will be seen in the Light.

It breaks my heart to see people put others on pedestals. We all deserve to value ourselves and believe in our own divine power. Although, it is to our benefit to honor the sacrifices and gifts others bring to the world. There are those, too, who play roles that model poor judgment and life decisions that we can observe while making our own choices. In either case, I've found it's wise to view others without excess adulation or critical judgment.

I'm aware that others act as mirrors for me. When I realize I'm finding fault with someone, it's a signal to me that there is most likely something similar I'm processing in my own growth. When I'm in turmoil with my own thoughts and judgments, I can recognize the pattern and remind myself that I prefer to remain in the Light. In that way I can forgive where necessary, release judgment of myself, and others while honoring my own healing.

It's helpful to remember that I attract what I need for my growth—my thoughts, the events and people in my life, are to be seen as opportunities and gifts. Therein lies the magic. I can choose to be asleep but it makes life so much more enjoyable and fascinating when I'm awake and aware as to what comes into my life and the beauty that is around me.

There are times when life can become exceedingly difficult. I recall, following my Kundalini awakening, when I was challenged with believing in myself and trusting in God. I'd chosen to face all of my unconscious fears while dealing with negative energies under very difficult circumstances. Moving through the darkness, clearing old thought patterns and fears brought me into the Light with greater clarity and understanding of my goals and myself. I came to understand that I am not my pain—that I could feel the contraction and darkness of my own being without fear, knowing that the Light was sure to follow. By the grace of God, I am free and clear now.

I'm reminded of the snake shedding its skin as we are transformed and rendered more solid, secure, confident, compassionate, and *awake*. The process, although sometimes painful, brings about empowerment and a new sense of self. Now my goal is not just to endure but also to maintain as much joy and contentment as possible, no matter what is occurring in my outer world.

Once while encountering a particularly difficult time, my Higher Power inspired me to write. What ensued was a poem called Transformation. I remembered how it surprised me that creative energy is available when we least expect it.

Indeed I discovered many tools to assist me through dark times. For example, when tempted to think negatively about myself regarding a particular situation, I simply say, "I'm not going there." I cancel the dark thought immediately while at the same time promising to be gentle and compassionate with myself.

Having a positive attitude implies having positive expectations. I'm aware that my intention helps to bring conditions about. As a result of my experiences, I now believe in "miracles." I know that my healing is available to me at any moment. Therefore, through my intent I can experience joy. I only need to surrender my situation to my Higher Power and release fear and judgment.

I remember one day I was experiencing emotional turmoil involving recurring thoughts and I decided to ask my Creator for inner peace. I was astounded to be awakened to the fact that I could pray for something and have my prayers answered immediately. Within seconds of my request I was at peace. I actually had a good laugh over it. "Is it really that easy?" I wondered. Being aware of what takes my joy away is also helpful. While noticing it, acknowledging it, and altering my consciousness, I can be in relief.

Further I discovered that often when I'm feeling down, I'm too much in my head and not in my heart. Moving into my heart-center takes me out of fear and into the knowledge that all is well even though outer circumstances may appear otherwise.

I choose not to live in melodrama, which is emotional and draining. Yet as always, it's progress, not perfection, and, I know my humanness moves me into fear of the unknown. Sometimes when the weather is dark and dreary, which it quite often is, I visualize myself, and others enjoying a beautiful sunny day. This scene helps pick up my mood and through my creation I not only help myself to feel better, I create my future as well.

Tunnel vision involving staring at the darkness can easily be remedied. I've found that by expanding my consciousness, thinking of others and doing whatever it takes to enlarge my perception, my world often changes as I learn to see it in the Light.

How often we forget about the magic and enchantment of all around us— both in the unseen world and in that which is apparent to us: a butterfly dancing near us, a cat brushing our leg, an unusual animal becomes visible to us, a bumper sticker on the car ahead of us brings a timely message. I love to be awake to appreciate such miracles.

Empowerment comes as I realize I'm deserving of the highest and best. I refuse to give my power away so that other people and conditions are unable to deflate my sense of well-being. Empowerment comes as I become aware of my goodness and how I can assist others. While coming to know myself, I'm able to express my essence in all that I do and through doing what I love, I may get in touch with my Spirit. When I believe in myself, others will believe in me also. Empowerment to me means discovering the value of finding self worth in just learning to be—to live and enjoy the moment!

Transformation

I've invited the darkness to join me
So that I may heal my past;
Together with angels of Light
I'm given a choice at last.

How I respond to life
Is entirely up to me.
I may follow the angels of darkness
Pretending I do not see,
Or I may go in faith and courage
If my wish is to be free.

I may judge myself and condemn my faults,
The choice is up to me,
Or I may look within the mirror
And honor what I see.

The way is never easy,
If your belief is strong.
For the tests will be intense
And the journey will be long.

I've invited darkness to join me
Instead of pushing it away,
So that I may clear my doubts and fears;
Not keep them just at bay.

And though I sometimes wonder
At the purpose of it all.
I know God has a plan,
For those who can recall
A time when they were troubled;
And things seemed more than they could bear,
To lift the hearts of others
And show them that they care.

Some come to pave the way
For those who come behind,
But to take the road less traveled
Leaves questions in the mind.

"Why me?" we sometimes ask.
"Why not?" the Voice replies.
God, with His sense of humor,
Our self-pity He denies.

And so the darkness lifts
As the angels of the night
Do their dance in the shadows
Of the angels of the Light.

Nurturing Mind, Body, and Spirit

I realized early on in life that I was powerless to control the events and people around me. I hadn't yet discovered the awareness and tools needed to assist me on my life journey.

Back in the '70s fear and anxiety began to cloud my life as my feelings of unworthiness caused me to abandon my faith in the God I so loved as a child. My frustration and anger concerning various conditions in my life only increased as I began to feel hopeless and trapped due to my lack of understanding that I needed outside help and support in dealing with the issues that confronted me on a daily basis. Much of my anger was directed inward for my inability to honor myself and make choices that were for my higher good. Thus my self-esteem suffered.

I was full of self-pity and remorse while seeking to blame others for my predicament because I hadn't yet learned to take full responsibility for my own thoughts, feelings and actions. How could it not be someone else's fault? I judged myself harshly due to what I saw as my mistakes and failures as I hadn't yet discovered the value and power of forgiveness. The vicious circle of addiction became my response to life's problems until such time I came to understand that I could choose to walk in Light and love for myself, and others.

During treatment when I discovered my new life, I put myself in God's hands. I had a vision of being on a train that was to take me to my new "home." Once on the train, there was no getting off. I would eventually reach my destination. There would be many stops and starts along the way and people would come and go and events would occur along my journey. However, through it all, progress would be made and my destiny was secure in spite of what outer circumstances seemed to predict otherwise.

I began to become aware of cycles during which time certain patterns would come up for healing. I would draw particular people and circumstances to me as challenges to see if this time around I would take the opportunity to respond to the situation in the Light. In other words I became aware of life's lessons that came and went. "This too shall pass" was a favorite expression of a wise friend of mine. I began to understand that nothing lasts forever and that in the blink of an eye things can change.

I began to see the wisdom of focusing on the positive in the understanding that my life was indeed my creation along with my Higher Power. It was, therefore, my responsibility to honor my abilities and my path as well as myself.

Surrounding myself with a positive support system was and still is important. My friendships involve others who are on a similar path of Light and healing. It is great fun to share with others who think similarly and see their life as a blessing and an opportunity to overcome their limitations and achieve their goals while learning to love themselves and others. Those on a spiritual path live consciously and are aware and awake to all that is around them. I am blessed with wonderful friends who are nurturing and inspire me to become all I can be. Those around us help us to grow as we observe and honor them for who they are and celebrate our similarities as well as our differences.

I know I can't fail when I focus on the Light in my life and in the lives of others. This takes me out of judgment while I observe with forgiveness, compassion and kindness my thoughts and feelings regarding myself, and others.

Early on in my, "new life" I came to understand that acceptance of my life conditions and myself was of utmost importance. I know that acceptance precedes change and that if things were going to change in my life; I had to accept everything just as it was in this moment. Early on it was about accepting my alcoholism which at first was painful for me until I came to see the wonderful gifts and blessings it brought to me; one of which was to learn not to take myself so seriously.

"Wear the world lightly," is an expression I like as it fits for so many occasions. I simply cannot find joy in my life if I'm taking it all too seriously. I love it when my angels remind me to lighten up and see the humor in things. It tells me that all is well in God's world.

Awareness that my Higher Power is in charge is beneficial particularly when I'm anxious about something occurring in a particular time frame. I need often to remind myself that our Creator looks after us and my patience may indeed be needed when events seem untimely and out of sync with my plans. Being human, I do not have all the information so I must trust in my Higher Power. When I truly believe this, I can remain calm knowing all is well.

I need also remind myself that I'm doing the best I can. On this journey in life I've often struggled with the feeling that I'm "late" with respect to accomplishing all I came here to do even though I'm not always sure exactly and precisely what that is. This is where I need to remind myself that I'm "on the train" and because I've consciously chosen to be on a spiritual path, I cannot fail. This is when my angels often come in and tell me to ease way up on myself. Once more I feel relieved and I can let go of my concerns.

My Creator also often reminds me to have compassion for myself. Embarking on my spiritual path I learned a lot about my faults and shortcomings as well as my gifts. However, because I was not accustomed to seeing myself in a positive way, I had a tendency to focus on that part of me that was not in the Light. Learning to love myself took time. I still need to be reminded by my angels as I struggle to view myself with compassion. Thank God I'm now seeing the blessings that come from loving myself, honoring my choices and having compassion for myself when I feel I may have failed and when I've merely misjudged myself. Progress for me is made when I let go of harsh criticism of myself, and others and view all with love and forgiveness.

My creation includes my desire to be my own best friend. That means I promise to honor and support myself while not judging my faults and acknowledging my gifts. I choose to cherish my being as one would a baby who is learning to walk. I can celebrate each new step that is taken and observe without judgment when I fall seeing all as progress on a path of Light. Unconditional love is the goal as I companion myself through life.

I am aware, too, of my thoughts as they are my creation. How I view my life and my challenges is important. I used to see my life as difficult and challenges as obstacles to my happiness and well-being. I now am aware that I can be in joy in spite of obstacles that come my way and can embrace the opportunities for healing and a closer relationship to my Creator. I may have moments at times of sadness, discouragement and fear. However, because of my understanding that we are all in God's care, I can go with the flow and tap into joy that I now see as a force within me that is always present and available to me!

Further, I know it's not what I do or do not do that is important but whether or not I am in the Light. Sometimes it's not about taking action, necessarily, but about just being. I believe we can help ourselves and others simply by being who we are. We all hold the energy of what we've experienced in our past. It relieves me to know, especially when I'm uncertain as to what to do, that I don't have to do anything except pray for the highest good for myself, and others. My past experience and my prayers are my gifts and that may be all that is required of me. This knowledge comforts me when I'm at a loss as to how to assist someone else.

Lastly, gratitude is an attitude that continues to nourish and sustain me. It aids me in climbing the ladder to becoming all I can be. There are times when I become aware of feeling discouraged and wanting more in my life that I am gently reminded to be grateful for what I have. There is a timing to everything and gratitude helps me to stay in the present as well as acknowledge the possibility of more abundance in the future. Gratitude brings me joy and relief to see how far I've come.

In order to thrive I need a nurturing environment in which to grow. It's important for me to surround myself with Light. I choose soft colors to accent the white in my environment and that helps to open my heart. I love blues, greens, rose and purples. Being sensitive I enjoy a setting where there is a flow to the energy. I also enjoy direct sunlight at least for part of the day.

My response to nature is such that I greatly benefit from the ability to be at one with the natural world simply by looking out the bay windows to the lawn and woods next to our house. I'm continuously amazed at the nature and wildlife we observe daily. How lucky we are! I also enjoy keeping things simple regarding the decor in our home. It helps me to maintain a calm and inner peace if my space is relatively neat and uncluttered.

It's vital as well, for my health and well-being, to take time out at least once during the day. Even five or ten minutes can be invaluable in how I choose to see myself and the conditions in my life. Thus my decisions are more apt to be made in the Light when I've taken just few minutes to rest periodically throughout the day.

Prayer and meditation are also valuable and necessary tools that help me greatly in achieving my goals and preventing me from feeling overwhelmed with the problems of daily life.

I view prayer as talking to my Higher Power and meditation as listening. As I was learning to meditate, I remembered that Jesus said,

"When you pray go into the closet and close the door." Well, I chose to use our fruit cellar in the basement as my meditation room. I lucked out. It was dark and quiet though a little cold and damp. I brought a candle into my little room along with a chair on which I sat with my hands folded in my lap. One day I drifted off only to catch the slight smell of something burning. I opened my eyes and noticed the candle was beginning to burn the shelf directly above it. Grateful that I'd been able to avert the tragedy of burning the house down, I was relieved of having to meditate in similar surroundings and took to communing with God in nature and higher ground.

I now meditate on my bed each afternoon that I'm able and it's usually around the same time each day. I use the same music that helps bring me "home" and at peace with my Higher Power and my guides and angels. I ask for divine protection to be placed around me and I may pray or just sit in the silence and trust in God's love and power as well as in my perceptions. My angels often talk to me or I may simply feel their presence. If my own thoughts or concerns intrude into my meditation, I merely brush them away like leaves blowing in the breeze. I do not judge myself during my time with my Creator. My meditation is not good or bad—it just is. I love this time of day, it brings me great benefit.

Another tool I value is journaling. I enjoy it because it helps to bring clarity to my thoughts and feelings. I believe journaling is a very personal thing and people use it in whichever way works best for them. Again I don't believe there is any right or wrong method.

Sometimes I benefit from giving myself an intuitive "reading." I "tune in" to my soul and look at the situation in question as best I can from my Higher Self. I'm often surprised at what comes. We are so much more powerful than we believe.

There have been times in my life, as with all of us that I've felt I needed extra support. These moments can surprise me, as I suddenly feel powerless in the wake of unfolding events. In the past I have envisioned a circle of divine beings and angels surrounding me as they send love into my heart. Invariably I feel nourished and enlightened with the divine energy that enfolds me.

Another gift that I learned in recovery is known as HALT. It is an acronym for *Hungry, Angry, Lonely* and *Tired.* The concept assists me in being alert to when any or all of these conditions are present. Taking time to breathe is very good for me. Over the years I have known this and yet have felt some resistance to putting it into practice. My yoga routine and meditation are two places where there is opportunity to focus on the breath. It's easy for me in my quiet times, but I have to remind myself to breathe when I become stressed and temporarily lose my center.

Being grounded has been a challenge for me especially in my past as I was going through extensive learning regarding the voices that plagued me. When I began to understand the meaning and purpose of it all, staying grounded came more easily to me. Fear used to cause me to become unbalanced, but I learned it would never destroy me.

Once again living in the Light and learning to nourish myself on all levels has been a wonderful gift to me. I discovered during my trials and challenges that watching TV or reading can be great tools for getting outside myself and forgetting my problems for a while. I've also learned that it's during this time that our guides and angels can work with us on subconscious levels. Many a time I've been made aware of solutions on pending issues following a TV program or reading a chapter in an engrossing novel. When I'm perplexed about something and need an answer, often I hear my angels tell me to read. I know this means they can enlighten me, as my emotions are not in the way. Oftentimes we seek answers and don't hear them because we are too emotionally invested in the outcome.

Similarly getting into a project is helpful. It's often when I least feel like working on something that it's the most valuable and beneficial for me unless, of course, I'm needing to rest instead. Many times I've been delighted to find that my mood picks up and my worries and concerns melt away as I engage in meaningful activity such as cleaning out a closet or organizing a drawer.

Using my time wisely is important to me. Making that a part of my intention each morning assures me that I will use my energy for the highest good. For example, when watching television there are times I prefer to simply rest, while at other times I may choose to expand my consciousness and engage in activities such as exercising, massaging my hands and feet, praying for others, or counting my blessings—all activities which benefit my health and nourish my soul.

Following my heart and intuition in making my choices brings joy and balance into my life, while staying in the Light allows me to go with the flow and be able to handle any emergency that may arise with grace and assurance that all is in divine order. Again it's progress, not perfection, and I only do the best I can.

Learning to counsel myself comforts and assists me. There are times when I am aware that the inner selves are talking to me. This used to be confusing but I now understand it. The various parts of ourselves want to have their say. For example I have the nun who is a no-nonsense being who exacts high moral standards from me. Then there is the monk who is kind, gentle, compassionate, and always sees me in the Light. Of course, we all have an inner child who often needs comfort and who encourages us to be more playful in our lives. The inner selves are often at odds with each other so it's important that I assume the role of boss.

There are times I'm not sure who is talking to me and I'll hear one of my guides say, "You're talking to the inner selves." That's when I know I need to stop listening and "take charge" of the situation by making my own decisions through listening to my intuition and following my heart.

Most people aren't necessarily aware of these inner selves. However, this is a challenge I chose for this lifetime—to be clairaudient and learn to discern, concerning the various voices that speak to me. Once I got past the fear and chose to stay positive and love myself through my challenges, my gift has brought me great wonder and joy! I'm no longer afraid as I've chosen to live in the Light.

Connecting with nature is very nourishing for me as it is for most people. When I go for a walk, I choose to be open in my heart to the various beings and nature spirits that inhabit the trees, flowers, greenery and wildlife around me. It transports me to other times and locations in this life and in other lifetimes.

Once again nature heals and brings me joy and balance. A walk, particularly after dinner, settles me down and calms me so that I may enjoy the evening ahead. During long walks I often use the tool of visualization to help create what it is I desire in my life. I create a scene in my mind, filling it with color and seeing it exactly as I want it to be. Then I breathe into it. I always add, "If this is for my highest good." My scene may be of me alone or may include others but it's always positive and in the Light. I've found these visualizations can bring very rapid results.

It's wonderful how, with our Creator, we can so empower ourselves.

Nourishment can also come through the help of friends and support groups as well as individual therapy. I've had experience with many forms of assistance. I find I learn best through encouragement. Support groups are helpful because in sharing my own experience, strength and hope, I can help others, and, as we know, in assisting others, we help heal ourselves. I also gain from hearing what others have to say. Invariably there is also humor and laughter, which is very healing. Sharing with others gets me out of myself and I find it time well spent.

Music is one of the most effective ways I nourish my soul. I've already talked about it so I won't say more except that I'm so grateful for all the various kinds of music that have been brought to me over my lifetime. From a small child to a teenager, and on throughout the years through playing the piano and singing in various choral groups, music has enhanced my life and shall continue to bring me Light, love and healing.

Nourishment comes to me also through my relationship to my husband, Tony. Sharing our lives in joy and sorrow, while being able to laugh at the ups and downs of everyday life, is a gift for which I'm eternally grateful.

Indeed I'm so grateful for all the ways my Higher Power has taught me to care for myself, while, through the support, knowledge and encouragement from others, I've been given many gifts to enhance my well-being. I hope that through this book others' lives will be blessed as well.

Learning Just to "Be"

Living in the moment,
Learning just to "Be,"
Following your heart…
Therein lies the key.

It's not about appearance
Or what you think of me,
It's not about being busy—
It's learning just to "Be."

We need not judge our present state
Though our energy be low,
Sometimes it pays to stop,
And learn to just let go.

So trust in your process,
And in your timing, too.
Learn to relax
Doing what you like to do.

You may take a walk,
Watch TV or read,
You may take a nap,
Whatever is your need…

For following your heart
And learning just to "Be"
Allows for greater things,
As in time you'll see.

So be kind to yourself,
And be gentle, too,
Look deep within…
Look to the inner you.

For believing in your heart
And learning to let go
Brings you to a space
Wherein new energies can flow.

New Light will emerge,
Trust yourself and you'll see.
Have faith in your Creator,
And allow yourself to BE.

Hope and Faith

Rev. Hutchinson, who was the minister of our church, visits me often, if not daily, from the spirit world. He used to say that faith is "knowing."

"Anything short of knowing is not faith." Faith in God is important as well as having faith in oneself. There are times I have faith in God, but not in myself. Other times I feel lucky and have faith in both.

Believing in myself has been a major issue for me. Consequently, I keep getting lessons in this area. Faith in God, however, has really been with me since I was a child and I don't believe that ever has been a real problem.

Learning to trust my Higher Power and the Universe in regard to the circumstances in life has been challenging. Believing that all will be well and that I won't be given more than I can handle, I feel, are tests that I've already undergone. I know that I'm always guided, safe, secure and divinely protected. This is not to say that I never have doubts. Basically, I trust in the Universe. I remain alert to messages that I know can come from anywhere and I know I get all the help and information I need.

Being willing to move beyond my fears and release the "what ifs" is still a challenge. I'm aware that nourishing doubt brings fear, while encouraging love and trust within myself will ultimately bring me peace.

My life experiences have taught me to have great trust in the concept of process. Yes, sooner or later I will get there as long as I create in the Light and stay in the solution as best I can.

There are times in my life that I need hope, which I believe means to wish or desire for something with some expectation that it will come about. We take a leap of faith but we need hope to bring us "to the edge." I need hope first, in order that I may have faith. Both are necessary to me for living my life and giving me the strength to accomplish my goals.

I tend to have faith with the larger circumstances in my life but lose trust and confidence in the small areas. For example, I tend to worry about the insignificant things. If I misplace my purse in the house, I panic and wonder whether I left it somewhere or if someone stole it. Also, being that I have been in several car accidents, not necessarily my fault, I tend to be fearful, especially in winter driving, feeling that an accident is "just around the corner." That, I discovered, is living in crisis mode. This awareness has given me a choice. I can choose to have the drama or let it go. For now, I'm working on it and happily I believe, most of the time, I'm strong in the Light.

I come by worry naturally. My grandmother was a worrier although she had reason. Several in her family died under tragic and unusual circumstances. My mother inherited the worry trait and passed it on to me. However, I really believe this is a pattern I brought into this lifetime to heal, so my mother is not the villain here. I alone am responsible, with God, to heal the issue.

With the larger issues I've had to deal with, I tend to evidence more faith not only in my Creator, but also in myself. For example, when I went to treatment in 1980 as my life began to unravel before my eyes, I knew I was going to be all right. I heard a voice tell me, "You are going to be just fine—even better than fine. Things are going to be very good for you." From that point on I relaxed and although I had my moments, I actually enjoyed my 28-day stint in rehab. After I got out, I immersed myself in recovery and "the program" in those early years, and was delighted with it, although I had the challenge of healing many old patterns that had been with me for a lifetime. It was indeed an adventure, and I'm very grateful for the opportunity, as it opened many doors for me.

My first surprise occurred upon my return home from the treatment center. I was feeling extremely vulnerable like a newborn bird. Tony and I had stopped to pick up something for dinner. I stayed in the car as the outside world was feeling a bit scary and overwhelming to me. As we entered our house I thought I'd check the mail. I received a letter from the University of Minnesota Duluth, the college I'd been attending on and off beginning at the University of Minnesota in Minneapolis. I was thrilled and astonished to read that, although I'd most likely been in a fog for some time while hitting my bottom with alcohol, I'd actually completed my degree! Yes, I graduated. Will wonders never cease!

Another significant time in my life that required a huge amount of faith had to do with my Kundalini experience and the resulting journeys into consciousness that lasted many years. At one point, I'd ended up in the mental health unit at Miller-Dwan Hospital. During my inner experiences, I felt divinely protected and secure in a profound way. On the other hand what I was experiencing was not "normal," to the average person's way of thinking.

My challenge, I felt, was to convince the psychiatrist I was not mentally ill but was having an "experience." This took a lot of faith in God and myself. I had visions of being misunderstood and locked up for good. However, because my Higher Power, spirit guides, and angels never left me, and made themselves known to me throughout my ordeal, I knew in my heart that I was at least at some level okay. Further, although I knew my condition was fragile, I always felt that there was a purpose to what I was experiencing and that it was all being directed by my soul. Upon looking back, I now embrace my adventure with love and Light, and honor its significance in my life.

Faith has expressed itself in countless and rewarding ways in my life. One beautiful fall evening I was lying on the couch in our sun porch staring out at the trees and I had the thought that I would just love to see a bear. I love bears—the small ones for their apparent cuddliness and the large ones for their magnificence. I sent out a prayer to my Higher Power that if it were for my highest good, please send me a bear. As long as I was safe in my house I could enjoy the bear without putting myself in danger. It was not long after, as I was watching TV, I heard Rev. Hutchinson, my dear friend in the spirit world, say to me, "Your bear is here." I looked out the window and, much to my surprise I saw a large black bear come lumbering through the woods into our yard. I sat up as I watched him come closer until he stepped up on our deck and pressed his nose to the glass door. I called for Tony. He sat in his chair just a couple of feet from the bear. I, on the other hand, became terrified and ran into the living room, all the while feeling guilty because it was I who had called the animal to me. Looking back, I knew I was safe; yet it was a natural instinct for me to run away. It's a wonderful memory, demonstrating faith in action and the importance of being ready to accept the responsibility for what you pray for.

Another illustration of hope and faith came when one day I heard my angels tell me, "It's important for you to make a Wish List, and *be specific*." This I did over a period of time and still add to it on occasion. My list constitutes that which I wish to create in my life. By reading this list often and staying in the Light on it through prayer and visualization, these conditions do indeed manifest in my life.

My Wish List thus becomes a life plan, like a road map, and alerts me and the Universe to what it is I desire in my life.

This has been a good experience for me. When I first heard my guidance on the Wish List, it struck me more like something out of a fairy tale rather than something religious or even spiritual. I also had a challenge in understanding that I do indeed "deserve" to have my dreams and wishes come true.

I'm very grateful for the Wish List. When I think of something or some condition, I want in my life, I simply add it to my list and of course, thank the Creator at the same time.

I don't read my list every day but when I do I'm astonished at how much of it, which is rather long, has manifested exactly as I had requested. I add to my goals with certainty now, as I know that if that which I've asked for is for my highest good, it will come to me.

I once had a very loving Light-Being tell me to think of her as a fairy godmother and imagine myself sitting on her lap telling her my troubles and asking for what I need in my life. The image was something I needed at the time and I felt very nourished and comforted. I know from these and many other experiences that through hope and faith, our desires can indeed become reality. We all need encouragement from time to time. I know I do. Once when I felt disheartened, I devised in my imagination a "hope chest." I filled the chest with hope and told myself I could draw from this energy any time. Being that thoughts are things in the spirit reality, I felt this actually would work for me. My intuition also told me I could use this for others who needed hope and encouragement. The energy would simply be there for them when they needed it. Occasionally I felt it was time to load up the hope chest again as it was getting low.

Another important tool in regard to Hope and Faith is prayer, which I find very beneficial. Prayers can be said at any time. There are prayers of gratitude and prayers in which we ask our Creator for what we need or desire. Sometimes I talk to my Higher Power while standing in a grocery line or while I'm driving. I definitely see a change in my life when I choose to expand the practice of prayer.

Simply talking to my Higher Power, expressing my feelings about issues and conditions in my life helps, as it becomes a form of therapy. Also I've found it extremely important and valuable to pray for others.

It's not only beneficial for them but helps to give me energy and expands my consciousness by including others in my thoughts.

Occasionally my intuition tells me it's time to write out a prayer. It's about getting it all out of my head and heart and on to paper. I use a 5 x 7 index card. That way everything I wish to pray for gets expressed. All I have to do is read it. Reading my prayer serves me for some time until conditions change and it's time to write a new prayer that reflects what is going on in my life at the time.

I believe in and don't hesitate to ask for "miracles," which are the result of working with God's energy at the highest vibration. I believe miracles occur if it's in the greatest good of all concerned. If they don't happen when asked for, I believe it simply means more learning is required. That way I can let go and trust in the wisdom of my Higher Power.

For many years I went to the Spiritual Frontiers Fellowship Retreat held at Carlton College in Northfield, Minnesota. It was always a great adventure and brought much joy to me. Spiritual teachers, psychics and healers came from all over the country. Every day we went to workshops of our choosing—one in the morning and one in the afternoon. We could also have psychic readings if we wanted assistance in that way and healings were always available at the Healing Center. For me it was a glorious time.

At the healing service held at the end of the week in the church on campus, there occurred what I would call a miracle. A young woman who had been coming to the retreat for several years and who had been legally blind, was healed. I used to see her each year with her cane and Seeing Eye dog walking to and from classes. This particular healing service was no different from the other services I'd attended. The healers were in front of the church and stood behind chairs that were lined up in several rows. The rest of the congregation was seated in the pews. Those who wanted healing would leave row by row and go up front and sit in the chairs behind a healer. It was very dramatic when the cry was heard, "I can see! I can see!" Truly a miracle had taken place. The young blind woman was cured and was seen the following year at the registration table helping people sign in. From what I know her cure was permanent. What a moment! I've never forgotten it. Obviously it was meant to be not only for the young woman, but also for the healer and for all of us who attended the service that day.

Regarding the world situation: we all need to have hope and faith. I've needed to understand that we all come from our own history both in this life as well as past lives. We also have our own beliefs based on the information we have been subjected to—not all of it valid or balanced.

I do believe we're all being called upon in different ways to assist the planet at this time. Therefore, we need to follow our hearts and intuition in this regard. I realize it's important that I refrain, as best I can, from getting into anger and fear regarding the news we're bombarded with each day. So what can I do? I know I can attempt as best I can to take the high road, recognize the drama and send Light and love wherever there is darkness and pain, when confronted with my own feelings of powerlessness. I also do whatever I can to stay centered and balanced while creating optimum health for myself (physically, mentally, emotionally and spiritually). I can focus on continuing to develop and maintain joy in my life and releasing all that no longer serves. This is a process and I need to be kind, gentle, compassionate, and forgiving of myself, and others. Progress, not perfection, is a good motto to follow here while keeping a sense of humor is essential for me.

I keep my list of things to be grateful for that I can read when I'd rather whine and complain. An attitude of gratitude opens the door for more blessings to come. In my experience there has always been opportunity where there is challenge and a gift where there is loss. "Trust" is the message I keep getting and know that all is working for the highest good.

Sometimes people have more faith in me than I have in myself. Back in the 1960s I had been invited by a family friend to be a page in the Minnesota State Senate. Politics was not my thing, but my soon to be husband, Tony, encouraged me to take the job. I was glad I did. It was fun and I met some great people.

One day I was sitting at the page's table feeling exhausted as I'd stayed out too late and celebrated too much the night before. The Bill Clerk, who had a very specific job, and who also sat at our table was absent that day and I was asked to take his place. I knew absolutely nothing about what the Bill Clerk did. At first I said, "No, I can't." No sooner had I said that when I heard, "Yes, Jill, I want you to be the Bill Clerk today." My prayer to God was quick and short. "Please, God, help me!" It was explained to me once what I was to do. Generally, I like to hear directions two or three times, if not more. So there I was standing before everyone taking care of the bills for the day. To this day I'm grateful it went well and I honestly don't know how it happened except that I know I was being given divine help.

On another day I was again seated at the table with the other pages and was asked if I would please help by holding up a very large heavy poster board as the Senate was about to discuss a sewer bill. Now I'm not a tall person. There were taller pages who could do this job with much more ease than I could. Feeling I had no choice, I stood there holding the board in front of the senate so all could see and I began to get the giggles. My arms became exhausted and I couldn't stop laughing. I waited, praying someone would relieve me, but no one came. The poster was shaking up and down. Eventually the senators began to chuckle. I peeked out from behind my poster and noticed most everyone was laughing. The discussion eventually came to a close—fortunately before I collapsed.

On another occasion the then Lieutenant Governor had asked me to watch his children who were there for the day. I felt honored and delighted and glad he had faith in me, although I was heading in a direction in which I was beginning to lose faith in myself. Life, with its ups and downs, had continuous surprises for me.

Lastly, I had a couple of wonderful experiences involving faith in regard to nature. Many years ago I went fishing with Tony. Actually he was fishing and I was just along to enjoy the day outdoors. We came to the spot where Tony chose to fish. He went down a slope and into a river while I chose to sit on a large rock up on a hill looking down on the stream. I thought it would be fun to meditate and to enjoy the early evening. However, there was one problem. The mosquitoes were horrendous. I knew instantly there was no way that I could sit there for five minutes, let alone an hour. I knew I had to do something. I asked my Higher Power to please protect me from the mosquitoes. I built my trust in God and was relieved to notice that there were indeed no mosquitoes in my midst. In my mind's eye I could see a large circle of protection around me. That was a demonstration of faith I think I needed at that time. I was greatly encouraged from that incident.

Jill Downs

Another similar situation occurred not too long ago when we were in Maui. I was sitting out on our lanai. It was nighttime and we had a light on the porch, which was great if one chose to read or write there later in the evening, which I often did. The space overlooked the beach and the ocean. I loved watching the palm trees sway in the breeze.

One particular night the bugs, being attracted to the light, were plentiful and bothersome. I told God I had planned to work on my book but could not with the distraction. "Please help!" I thought of the time years ago with the mosquitoes and felt myself in the same circumstances. I was elated to see the bugs disappear so I could write. I felt enormously humbled and gratified with these situations. We are so loved and cared for by our Creator.

Trust in Your Creator

Trust in your Creator
And know you can be healed
Of all your doubts and fears
Which you have held concealed.

Trust in your Creator
To know where shadows hide.
And as He does expose them,
In His love abide.

For if you trust in God,
And know you are secure,
You will be surprised
At what you can endure.

And as you face your tests,
Your inner strength will grow
Until your fear does vanish
Like the winter snow.

Trust in your Creator
And look forward to the spring,
When you will feel much lighter
And your soul begins to sing.

Trust in your Creator
Know all is His design.
Know that you are learning
Within yourself resign.

For as you trust in God,
He will be your friend.
And though it seems too much
For you to comprehend.

Trust in your Creator
For He knows what's best.
And you can go within the flow
Passing every test.

Trust in your Creator
Right up until the end
And you will be so grateful
That you've come to depend

Upon the greater Source,
Upon the God you've come to trust
And you will be rewarded;
It's a promise—it's a must!

Service

My views on service were formed early in my childhood as my mother was very active in our community. She was president of the Junior League and, for as long as I remember, was on various boards and held many volunteer positions around town. I was always aware of her feelings on the benefits of helping in the community.

At her encouragement I joined the League and was there for eleven years until I realized I needed a change and decided to go to school instead, which I continued to do on and off for many years.

However, I did, throughout my life, serve in various groups and organizations and was indeed grateful for the opportunity. To name a few... I've taught Sunday School, served on the Miller Dwan Hospital Chemical Dependency Board, facilitated groups in recovery at the Treatment Center and led meetings at the County Jail. I've been a docent at several museums including the Railroad Museum, Tweed Museum of Art and Glensheen Mansion. I've also volunteered at hospitals and nursing homes in various capacities from being a Candy Striper to working with the elderly and dying at Hospice. Further I've served as Board President of our church and taught meditation classes there as well as in the community. I'm very grateful now to my mother who set the example for me regarding the benefits of being a volunteer as it brought me many wonderful experiences and gave me some needed structure at that period in my life.

There came a time however, when I realized I served myself, and others best when I followed my heart and decided to create and present my own workshops on personal and spiritual growth. I chose to gather my courage and view my life processes from a higher consciousness so that I might help others who had similar patterns and gifts as I had. This was a great joy to me—to share knowledge and experience from my own life journey. It was also very healthy and transforming.

In 1999 my book entitled *The Awakening of the Heart* was published. Having been inspired by my Higher Self, it explores many areas of life and death. Much time had elapsed since the first writing of the work until its publication. The intervening years were necessary so that I might process and integrate the information contained in the book. I feel the information is as pertinent today as it was when I initially wrote it. As with many others who write, the process entailed much faith and perseverance to see the project to its conclusion.

When our daughter, Cindy was going to school at the University of Colorado at Boulder, I used to go out and visit her quite frequently. It was something I always enjoyed. On one of these visits when I was driving along a winding road by myself, I began to think about my life and how nice I had it—how comfortable I was.

I had, in the past, been presenting my workshops, doing volunteer work, etc., but everything I did for others was on my time and to my liking and for my convenience. I began wondering if I would stop to help someone when they needed it as in an emergency.

Shortly after having these thoughts, a young woman seemed to come out of nowhere. She appeared to be half staggering alongside of the road holding on to her stomach as if in great pain both physically and emotionally. I stopped and asked her if she needed help. She said, "Yes!" We both agreed she needed to go to the hospital. I got her there and into the care of those who would be treating her.

I knew my part was over except to send her Light and love, which I did. I never found out what was wrong; only that she had been very ill at the time. Later on, my intuition told me that she was all right. It was comforting for me to know I was willing and able to help her. I was grateful for the experience and needed the affirmation that I would take the opportunity to move out of my comfort zone to assist someone else. The Universe did indeed respond to my inquiry.

On another occasion while in the grocery store, as I was pondering my life, I was awakened to the fact that I wasn't "out there" and "busy" doing service work. I was no longer presenting my workshops or volunteering in any noticeable fashion. This was upsetting me and I started to feel somewhat guilty about it.

Almost immediately after asking my Higher Power for a "sign" to lead me in the right direction, I "just happened" to run into an old friend I had known years ago but hadn't seen in some time. We had shared much together on our spiritual journeys throughout the years. She informed me that she had just attended a workshop given by a wonderful spiritual teacher she'd known for some time. He had talked about how it's the little everyday things that matter. It's the taking advantage of the small opportunities that come our way to uplift others that is important. People tend to think of success as the large accomplishments when it's often the small things that make up our day that count.

That's not to say that the more focused, obvious ways of doing healing work are not important. They truly are. However, I needed to get the message that encouraged me to continue to relish my private life and tend to my own self-awareness and healing. I was exceedingly grateful to my friend for being my teacher and angel that day.

I also visited with a therapist with many years of practice who once told me that it's good for everyone, she felt, to take a break from public service, as people need to learn how to "just be" and nourish themselves. There comes a time when we all have to slow down either because of sickness or old age. My friend said that it's those people who have periodically taken time off from being continually busy working with others and having an exceptionally active life that have an easier time making the transition either into retirement and old age or being released from the body through death.

So what can I do to take advantage of the small opportunities that come my way? How can I learn to "just be" and still be able to assist others? I've found it's the smile given to a stranger or a hug to a friend who needs encouragement. It's the kind word to the cashier in the grocery store who obviously feels harassed and tired. It's the healing thought sent to someone who is ill. These are the standards by which we can choose to live up to on a daily basis. Indeed there is much in the way of service we can perform simply living day to day.

Thus, I discovered it's important to honor my own life process. This "time out," to my astonishment, and later gratitude, took years. Again after my Kundalini opening and resulting journey into consciousness, I felt that I was neglecting my service work, forgetting that my experiences in and of themselves were part of my service as well as my joy.

I was told by those Light-Beings who watch over me that I needed to rest. REST? From what? I didn't feel "tired." I now understand our Higher Power knows when it's time to relax, to unwind and to enjoy nature. High vibrational energy is useful, stimulates us and helps us get things accomplished. However, it needs to be released from time to time.

Often we feel let down following its release. High intensity energy takes a toll on us whether we're aware of it or not. My decision to slow down, I feel, benefits me as well as others and I am free to totally enjoy my life in freedom, relaxation, and joy.

I do have a healing list that is not an actual list on paper but is in faith. I ask that the angels record the individual names I request to be put on the list. In other words God keeps track and does the healing.

Occasionally, when it feels appropriate, I tell people about my list and they are then given the choice of whether or not they wish to be on it. Sometimes I encounter someone whom I feel might like the healing and I preface my request to God with, "Only if it's for their highest good." This way it is not in my hands. In other words, again, the choice is up to their Higher Power and not up to me. I also ask that people be taken off the list when it's best for them. If an individual is not ready for a healing at a particular time when the healing is sent, the energy is not received.

I love my healing list. I ask that healing be sent to the entire list at least once each day. It helps to balance my energy. I'm aware I receive a great deal of help every day and in this way I can send out love and healing in return. I'm told at night, during sleep, I check on my list and verify it according to spiritual law.

Since I was a child, I've always had the inclination to bring healing to others who are suffering. Along with my healing list throughout the day, I am intuitively inspired to send love and Light to those who are in need. Divine guidance is given to me whether it is preferred that I send the energy myself, or ask Higher Power to please send the healing.

Everyone has gifts to contribute to humanity. I'm very grateful to be able to use my gifts in this way. It provides me with an opportunity to serve that I can accomplish anywhere and anytime. In this way I live in great abundance as the circle of energy of giving and receiving is continual and beneficial to myself, and others.

In the spirit world we have opportunities to help as well. One of the services I enjoy doing is assisting people in making their transitions.

Usually I do the work during sleep time. However, once, while in Maui, I was in a restaurant with Tony having dinner. I'd been having a wonderful time on my trip and was feeling like I needed to be giving back the joy I'd been so blessed to receive.

I had gone into the rest room and became aware of the spirit of a young woman who was talking to me. She said, "I just died." She was obviously frightened and very angry. She had overdosed on drugs and found herself lost in the Spirit World. Throughout the meal, while in conversation with Tony, I mentally talked to her, telling her to call on her angels and Higher Power. I did the same for her. She then told me she was in a very beautiful cathedral. Her voice was totally changed. I knew she was in good hands and in the Light. I thanked God for taking care of her.

Normally this doesn't happen to me under such circumstances so as to interfere with my life. However, I had asked to be of service, and I was told that those Light-Beings in charge of the situation said that, because my heart was open and I was in the Light, I could handle it.

As I was leaving the restaurant, I heard a Light-Being say to me, "Now do you feel like you've done something worthwhile?" After that I felt satisfied with "just being" and enjoying the trip while continuing to send prayers and healing to others.

I'm grateful for the opportunities that come my way to serve. I especially enjoy going to visit our daughter Cindy, her husband Lazlo, and their wonderful family in Colorado including their eight-year-old triplets. Tony and I like to help out where we can.

I greatly enjoy our stays there and am honored and blessed by the opportunity to participate in their lives. I take immense joy and appreciation in being able to bond with each of the children. I tell them how much we love them and watch their eyes light up. I believe each child is a miracle. I'm extremely proud of them and love them with all my heart. We watch them grow and delight in their changes. We also find them very amusing. I've been keeping a small book of "Kid's Quotes" for the family to enjoy as the children get older. We also enjoy their dogs, Cubby, a Bernese Mountain dog, and Biggens, a wonderful black dog of mixed breed (mostly Lab). We also miss Sarah their German Shepherd as well as their Golden Retriever, Molly, who died at the ripe old age of eighteen.

There is never a dull moment there as you might imagine, with school and all the other non-stop activity. I never fail to notice the silence at our house upon our return home. I feel honored and grateful to be a part of it all. Indeed, opportunities to serve abound when I'm in the Light.

Answered Prayer

Yes, I'd been down and feeling blue,
And then I got the call from you.
Your words were kind and touched my heart.
'Twas like a plan right from the start.

Encouragement is what was needed,
And the angel's voice you heeded
Giving to me what I needed to hear,
Helping as well to release my fear.

Earlier that day I'd sent out the thought
In the form of a prayer—the way I'd been taught.
"I need hope," I said, "and confidence, too,
And anything else for me you can do."

In my mind's eye the angels I see,
Talking to you as you talked to me.
You relayed the message the angels had brought
Believing, of course, it had just been your thought.

So listen for angels and heed their advice.
You, too, have the chance to do something nice.
For as we help others our aura we brighten,
And as we give out, our load we lighten.

Opportunities come and go every day.
Angels among us help pave the way.
If you feel impressed to say something kind,
It may be an angel's voice in your mind.

We all need encouragement—compliments, too.
We need to feel good about all we do.
So open your heart as I know you care.
You may be the answer to somebody's prayer.

Living With Joy

It's wonderful how we can create, with our Higher Power, our own methods for taking care of ourselves. There was a time in my life when I felt overwhelmed with psychic activity and spirit voices. I devised a system that helped me to feel more secure and comfortable. I imagined three switches: one to the left of me for grounding; one in front of me for cleansing the aura and mending tears or holes in my energy field; and the third switch, that, when turned on, would place me in a bubble of protection—the color of which I would leave to my Higher Power depending on what I needed at the time.

I would turn on my imaginary switches in the morning in the belief that they did indeed work for me. One day as I was doing my yoga, I heard a spirit guide say, "You forgot to turn your switch off. You need to turn it off." With that information I devised an automatic shut-off system. This seemed to work well.

Another tool I have used to aid in making decisions is an imaginary meter with numbers ranging from one to ten. If I'm having difficulty deciding the best course of action for something, I first make sure I am in the Light. I then ask my Creator for divine protection as I visualize the needle going from one to ten in order to "charge" my meter. I then ask my question. Where on the scale does the needle fall? I can also use it with a "Yes" or "No" answer if I'm wondering whether or not taking action on something is in my highest interest.

Co-creating with the God of my understanding has brought me other gifts. Though we have no pets, Tony and I attracted to us tame foxes. I had one I called "Foxie" who came several times a day. Yes, we did feed her only after I prayed for guidance on the issue of feeding a wild animal. My intuition told me it was in the Light for both the fox and us.

I became so attached to Foxie. She was adorable and I loved her. She would come running out of the woods when I whistled and called for her. Sometimes she wanted food while at other times she would be content to sit in the sun with me on our deck. She brought me great joy and I grieved for a long time following her death.

Later on I saw her spirit several times in our house. One time she was with a guide coming out of our bedroom. Another time I saw her in our dining room. It gave me great comfort to know she was aware of how much she was loved.

Several years later we attracted three foxes—a mother and two kits. They were with us through the spring and summer. They would come every day and romp and play in the yard. They were very tame.

One evening I sent a telepathic message to Foxie II, as I called her, when we were out having dinner with another couple. I asked her if she would come to our house because our friends wanted to see her. Sure enough, there she was on our front walk. She usually came to the other side of the house so her appearance there was unusual. She looked at me as if to say, "Well, I'm here! Now what?"

One of the gifts of the three foxes was to give me hope that new ones could indeed come again and although they could not be replaced in my heart, I didn't grieve so long after nature decided that I would see them for the last time.

Enjoying life as I was, I came to the realization that I desired to make joy a priority in my life and that I wanted to learn to pursue my goals without fear. To my delight, through learning to follow my heart and intuition while trusting in my Higher Power, I've been enjoying creating a new reality based on joy.

I now begin the day by thanking God for all of my blessings. I then ask my Higher Power to please send love, healing, and divine protection to all of my loved ones and to those who are on my healing list. My intention includes my desire to be strong in the Light and to use my energy for the Highest Good throughout the day.

I then set my "vibrational channel" to joy by "remembering" what it feels like to be happy and be at one with myself. My goal then is to follow my heart and "tune in" to how I may create to bring joy to my life that day.

Yes, there are days I have to do things that challenge my ability to be in joy. Going to the dentist, for example, gives me an opportunity to practice staying in a joyful place when my tendency may be to become anxious about my upcoming appointment. I'm fortunate as I'm very fond of my dentist and confident in his work. However, I always say a prayer asking that we be in divine Light during our time together. That way everything turns out for the highest good and I most often leave the office in joy and gratitude.

I have been greatly blessed in my life—my family being that which I cherish the most. Tony and I take trips to Colorado several times a year and always over the holidays with our daughter, Leila, when she is able to come. We greatly enjoy seeing Cindy, Laszlo and the triplets.

Travel is an important part of our lives, especially our annual trip to Hawaii. Maui, for me, is a magical place with a generally predictable lovely climate, gorgeous beaches, healing ocean waters, and sunny days. Upon arrival there as I absorb through all my senses the tropical Maui air, there is a rush of excitement that runs through me and I feel as though I have come home. I love walking the nearly deserted beach that often becomes busy as the local fisherman set up their tents at the state park near our condominium to enjoy the weekend. I especially enjoy watching the children swim and play in the sand while the adult's fish and prepare food for the next meal. Tony always says, "You can tell if it's going to be a nice weekend if the tents are up," which is as good a forecast as any.

Another favorite pastime while on our lanai is watching the whales breaching and slapping their tails. One day Tony and I were walking the beach while a mother whale and her calf were swimming along side of us. The loud and very primal sound coming from the whale sent shivers through us.

I also greatly enjoy going to the swap meet—a colorful and ever popular outdoor market held on Saturday mornings. Many of the vendors have been there for years. For example, there's the gifted composer whom I've gotten to know having bought all of his wonderful CDs that are great for yoga, meditation, and relaxation.

There's also the talented artist whose paintings now hang in our home. I have a friend at the market whom I've known for years who designs clothes that are always very popular. Then there's the gal who designs her own line of jewelry. I enjoy buying clothes for our grandchildren there because they are made from colorful Hawaiian prints, sold at a decent price and the kids love them.

There's just about everything you can imagine at the swap meet. Tony looks at the fruits and vegetables while I check out everything else. I also often unwind by receiving a short massage from one of the several body workers who are there. I never tire of the swap meet. I am also filled with joy and wonderful memories of body surfing with Leila both at "our" beach and at McKenna Beach where the waves are very high and awesome. We had an audience of several people watching us from the beach. We got laughing so hard that we could barely get out of the water as the undertow kept pulling us backward. These are the memories I cherish from Hawaii.

Maui sunsets are "the best," marking the end of yet another beautiful day. At night I sit on our lanai and absorb the moon's reflection on the ocean as the waves roll in, calming me while letting me know all is well. I pray for others as I watch the stars and the lights twinkling on the opposite shore. I feel safe and secure with gratitude in my heart as I fall asleep with the soft island breezes lightly touching my face.

I am grateful that, no matter where I choose to be, my Higher Power along with my spirit guides and angels are always with me. Further, it is with joy that I bring news from the spirit world that our friends and loved ones do survive the transition called death into a new life beyond the veil.

I often receive messages from those who have "died" to let me know they are in good hands and being cared for by those on the other side. Many quite rapidly begin their new life in the spirit world. They tell me they are celebrating with others and are happy and content while discovering the joy of realizing their dreams.

Following one's death, there appears to be a period of adjustment to life in the spirit world after which those who have made their transition sometimes begin to assist those on earth who have similar issues and challenges that they themselves had during their lifetime. There is divine help available in the spirit world as well. It's my belief that there are ample opportunities to learn through counseling, classes, and "support" groups in the spirit realm just as we have here on earth.

Enlightenment comes to those who seek God whether here or on the other side. I ask for divine help often with my endeavors. I've discovered that, in every area of my life, there are Light-Beings available to assist any undertaking. No matter how small or insignificant the request may seem, my Higher Power, through spirit, is always there when I ask for divine assistance.

My Creator brings me countless blessings through my spirit guides and helpers whom I've learned to trust. The divine beings and angels who assist me know and understand my goals, so they often come to assist me by bringing me messages of love and encouragement, while reminding me that I'm not alone in the world. They respect my privacy and touch my heart with their kindness while teaching me to believe in myself.

My spirit helpers assist me through troubling waters by reminding me to pray for others when I'm upset and to see myself in the Light in all situations. They also encourage me to stand on my own two feet when I become too reliant on those in spirit for information and guidance. I became almost child-like for a while when this gift of clairaudience unfolded. Therefore, I needed to learn to listen to my intuition, follow my heart and to believe in myself once again. It became important that I not judge my process, but love myself while learning to live in both worlds.

One of the ways in which my spirit helpers assist me is to help me to lighten up. They encourage laughter and help me to see the humor of various situations. If I tend to start worrying unnecessarily about my health, for example, they respond by getting me laugh at myself. They advise me of the wisdom of finding humor in the events and circumstances of my life.

Humor helps me to stay in the Light and live in the solution while not taking myself so seriously. It helps me to own and laugh at my mistakes and to accept my humanness and limitations. One of the gifts in recovery is the way we can often laugh at ourselves and events in our past that others would find tragic.

Humor also helps me to maintain a sense of balance and brings perspective to my life. It assists me in being open to see the silver lining in the clouds and the opportunities that come with the challenges that confront me on a daily basis. I can learn to see the positive side of every situation and can understand what I'm learning from a particular experience without allowing it to consume me.

Having humor means I can accept myself as I am and others as they are without judgment. Accepting myself, and life as it is while taking things lightly and acting responsibly, I can prepare myself for the challenges ahead. Having humor means I can be myself.

I'm so fortunate my guides and helpers in the spirit realm are often very funny. Their humor brings me great joy and health. I often find myself laughing out loud as they come to brighten my day.

Along with maintaining a sense of humor in order to be happy on this earth, I'm aware I need to honor my past. My history is important to me because it brought me to where I am today. It's essential that I forgive myself and not judge my mistakes. I'm aware that all is for my learning and to my ultimate benefit.

Exploring the beauty and richness of my life and past associations brings me peace because I know each experience and relationship has brought me closer to my Higher Power and in alignment with a more joyful existence than I have previously known. Allowing for my successes as well as my "failures," I have learned to love and care for myself. Out of my past come hope and trust in the future.

Further, living a joyful life, for me, includes surrendering my will to my Higher Power while believing in myself. It implies acceptance of life on life's terms while understanding challenges as opportunities that, if faced in the Light, will ultimately benefit me as well as others. In other words I acknowledge that I am not a victim, nor am I powerless. I'm always given a choice.

I have the opportunity to practice peace and handle stress in new and creative ways rather than falling back into old patterns.

A new attitude of faith and trust can enable me to stay in the solution. I believe there are no "bad" choices, only decisions either made in the Light or chosen for my learning. I'm aware that my choices are not about what others think or do, but what is right for me. Today, it's not about being "the good girl" but about coming from a place of Light, honesty, and following my heart.

Awhile back I'd been having trouble with various aches and pains including sciatica. I had been to several practitioners without much luck, though they were kind, professional, well informed, and gave me exercises designed to help me.

I always had the feeling the pain would eventually go away but I was growing impatient with myself and wanted to know when and how I was going to recover. Due to my discouragement with my condition, I was beginning to feel hopeless. Tony was kind and patient with me, but I knew I needed to change my attitude.

I realized, when outside help wasn't working as I had expected, I made a decision to join with my Higher Power and work on this from my heart. With assistance from the Master Jesus, Archangel Raphael (the healing angel), other healers from the spirit realm, and faith in myself and my massage therapist, who does healing work as well, I'm now on the road to recovery.

My guidance tells me it's essential to stay in the Light on my healing. It also benefits me to keep up with my prayer and meditation which gives me information concerning my condition while journaling helps me to process my feelings and experiences.

I've learned to draw the healing energy into my body while releasing all judgments, worries and fears concerning my health and my life. Visualization plays a key role as I see my body in the Light and free of pain, which I decided I did not need.

Through my prayers I send healing to others, as I know this is important to my own recovery. Sometimes I talk to my body and reassure it that it's safe to let go and release the tension that is held there. Following my intuition and my heart has given me faith and trust in my own tools and process of healing.

I'm learning to be gentle with myself. My intent is to do the best I can while not judging the outcome. My goal is to honor all that I choose to create and explore in this life while living in acceptance and joy with the challenges and opportunities that present themselves to me.

Further, I have the choice as to how I see others. I prefer to view all with compassion and respect, for I'm not in a position to judge anyone's path.

I'm grateful as well for the freedom to choose how I spend my time. I desire to use my energy each day for the highest good, and my gifts and talents to assist others, however that manifests at different stages of my life.

I choose to surround myself with a loving space that is protective, nurturing, and Light-filled. I desire to maintain special bonds with my husband, children and grandchildren whom I thoroughly enjoy while maintaining a network of friends who are enjoyable and love to laugh.

I'm in gratitude to God and all who walk with me whether in the physical realm or in spirit. I'm especially grateful to my guides and angels whose love, inspiration and humor help sustain me through my life, and will carry my forward until it's my time to make my transition.

In order to be in joy I know I also need to hold the belief that through the Creator all is possible. From a young age I've always had the feeling that my material needs would be met. I now understand how holding that belief is essential in all areas of my life including my health.

I used to feel that pleasing others was one of my main goals in life. My experience has now led me to believe that it's not only okay but also beneficial to me as well as others to make enjoying myself and being happy my main priority, and with that, comes certain awarenesses and responsibilities.

For example, it's important that I understand that I have a purpose in life, and following my heart helps me to see what that is, and how I can choose goals that are in line with my talents and abilities. In order to realize my dreams, I need to help others achieve theirs through being in the Light, while giving hope and encouragement when needed. If I want success for myself, I need to celebrate the accomplishments of others.

This can be a challenge and often demands patience, courage, and understanding. I've discovered that the attitude of comparing myself to others is not wise. We don't always have all the information and we may be learning different things. My goals include loving myself as I am and supporting myself through my processes.

Each day I pray for the highest and best for myself, and others. In order to be abundant it's important that I see failures as stepping-stones to success. It helps me to understand that as long as I remain on the spiritual path, I can trust in God's timing and not get upset when I fear I have failed. Other opportunities will surely come for me to "get it right," and, as they say, I have "all the time in the world" to heal my issues.

Further, in order to enjoy the blessings of the Creator, I need to be thankful for what I have. When I find myself in distraction concerning the mundane annoyances and pressures of daily life, I realize it's time to remember to be grateful. Gratitude is essential to an abundant life and taking time to count my blessings changes my attitude and brings me to joy once again.

Being in abundance-consciousness means also that I must give back in order to receive. I can choose to donate goods, services, and money. I can give of my heart, my time, and my energy. I can use whatever gifts and talents I have toward contributing to life. Simply living in Light and joy helps raise the consciousness level of mankind. Understanding that abundance is a state of mind is helpful to me because I'm able to recognize when fear takes me out of the flow.

Believing that "I deserve," and learning to receive on many levels and in many areas of my life has been a life-long process. Many of us grew up in the belief that in order to be a good person we must always put others first. Looking after my own needs and learning to take care of myself through loving myself and nourishing my spirit came later in life. I now know that in order to live an abundant life in God consciousness, I need to allow permission to feel, and to give to myself, that which I may look to receive from others.

As part of my healing and choosing to live in the Light, I enjoy playing with color. For the most part my clothes are quite colorful. I choose whatever I wear based upon how I feel. All colors have a vibration, and as a result, bring different benefits to me—depending on my own energy.

For example, I wear red when I feel energetic and outgoing; turquoise when I wish to enjoy the healing energy and good luck it brings and blue when I feel peaceful. I enjoy wearing purple because I benefit from the high vibration. Yellow reminds me of the sun and is a happy color, while green, to me, represents growth and stability. I wear pink when I'm full of joy and peace. I find it in my best interest not to wear black if I'm not at my best. However, if I'm strong in the Light, black is fine.

I think it's great fun to experiment with color. Wearing those colors that complement and blend with my own energy benefits me. However, it's important to remain positive on whatever choice I make.

Another gift of healing occurred for me one day as I happened to look out the window and noticed a flock of birds sitting in a tree. There were so many of them that I found it interesting and continued to stare at them. Then suddenly they all flew away together. However, one of the birds "turned into Light" and flew into our house.

My spirit guides told me my path of awareness was increasing and I needed to see how life continued after the spirit leaves the body. I was very grateful for the gift, as it was a miracle I needed at the time. I was told that the bird would bring me joy. How fascinating it would be for us to be aware of all the invisible gifts that we attract to assist us from the spirit world.

On another occasion when I was in a department store dressing room, I became suddenly aware of an energy unlike anything I had ever experienced before. It felt like a very high vibration that "quivered" and danced around me. It spoke saying, "I am the *Holy of Holies*." I was in total awe and utter amazement! Isn't one usually in a sacred space in the presence of lighted candles and incense to attract such Light? I thanked the divine energy for coming, and wasn't ever quite the same upon leaving the dressing room. I later asked why this energy came to me and I heard, "Because you were open to it." I am in profound gratitude to this energy for presenting itself to me not only because it brought me great joy, but because it taught me that miracles can indeed happen to us anytime and anywhere if we are willing and open to receive. I am elated to tell you the *Holy of Holies* comes to me now as I write about it.

Throughout all of my experiences, inner turmoil, and the ups and downs of everyday life, I've come to the conclusion that joy is a force, like love, which is always present. It is the feeling deep down within me that tells me I'm grateful to be alive.

I know now that my moods of happiness or unhappiness are transitory and that joy can be a permanent state when I choose to tap into it. I am blessed with the knowledge that the state of being joyful can be anyone's as there is no law against being happy. When we have discovered the ability to be in joy, in spite of what is going on around us, we have truly accessed the divine within ourselves.

My Inner Child

My little one
You are so small.
You look to me
Just like a doll.

Can you hear me?
Can you see?
I talk to you…
Please talk to me.

I've ignored you all these years,
And now it's time to dry the tears.
The time has come for you to heal;
The time has come for me to feel.

I've put it off now long enough.
Oh, I've been brave and I've been tough;
But now the time has come for you
To share with me what you've been through.

So talk to me, my little one
And I promise I won't run.
I'll be here right by your side;
Trust in me and please don't hide.

It's okay to make me sad,
And it's okay to make me mad.
I'm ready now, bring on the rain.
I'm ready now to feel the pain.

I know you're honest, this I trust
I know your fears and they are just.
I'm ready now to see what's real
To know just how I really feel.

Without you I could not grow.
I need your wisdom, this I know.
Little one, please speak to me,
Without you, I can't be free.

I need your little hand in mine,
I need your truth, your love divine,
I need your trust, I need your smile,
I need to know that I'm worthwhile.

And after all is said and done,
Let's go out and have some fun.
You can show me how to play
— how I can enjoy the day.

I know through you that I can learn.
You can help me to discern,
Honesty is what is needed,
Signals deep inside are heeded.

Free expression, from the heart.
Honesty is but a start.
Love is waiting at the door.
Peace, at last forever more.

Acknowledgments

Along with family and friends in both the physical and spiritual worlds, I'd like to thank my guides, angels, and teachers, who lovingly assist me in my life.

I'd like to also thank my publisher and wonderful friend Mike Savage who saved the day and made my dream a reality.

I'm hugely grateful as well to my long-time kind and trusted friend Richard Bellamy, who through his many unique talents and gifts, assisted me in my healing process and through his work with kinesiology, helped me to affirm my choices for the ideas and inspiration in this book. He is an educator and kinesiologist and can be located at kineticed@juno.com.

I'm also grateful to Kim Luedtke—"Coach, clairvoyant, and creative genius," for her truly remarkable gifts, her humor, and friendship. She's been an invaluable source of insight and encouragement. Her email is luedtkek@hotmail.com.

I'm also very thankful for Barbara Wood—a true "Angel Lady," friend, gifted clairvoyant, and spiritual counselor who has assisted me in believing in myself, encouraged my process with this book, and brought joy to my life. Barbara lives in Naples, Florida, and can be located at barbarajwood@juno.com.

I'm grateful as well to Deb Walli whose kind words, loving support, and gift of intuition has been especially helpful to me. Her email is walli_deb@yahoo.com.

Special thanks go as well to Margaret Manderfeld, our wonderfully talented cover artist, whose patience and understanding of my need for "process" made her an absolute joy to work with.

Thanks to Beth Grbavcich for her publishing assistance and to Debbie Zime for her valuable contribution with the lay-out of my book.

About the Author

This is Jill Downs' second book. Her first, *The Awakening of the Heart,* has ministered widely and often to diverse readers nationwide. Jill has a B.A. in sociology and has worked as a Licensed Practical Nurse (LPN), has facilitated family groups in recovery and has experience working with the elderly in nursing homes and the dying in hospice. She has created and facilitated workshops on personal and spiritual growth. She has served as Board President of the Lake Superior Interfaith Community church and was instrumental in creating a learning center there. Her intuitive skills were developed through work in spiritual counseling and teaching meditation classes in the community. Her spiritual growth and development has included a significant spiritual awakening with profound journeys into consciousness and intensely challenging work on the inner planes. Her intent is to live consciously, to be in her heart, and to love life and all it has to offer. Jill lives with her husband on the shore of Lake Superior in Duluth, Minnesota. They are blessed to have a daughter living in Duluth and another daughter, son-in-law, and wonderful 8-year-old triplet grandchildren living in Colorado. Her email is: downs.jillm@gmail.com.

Other Savage Press Books

OUTDOORS, SPORTS & RECREATION

Cool Fishing for Kids 8-85
      by Frankie Paull and "Jackpine" Bob Cary
Curling Superiority! by John Gidley
Packers "verses" Vikings by Carl W. Nelson
The Duluth Tour Book by Jeff Cornelius
The Final Buzzer by Chris Russell

ESSAY

Awakening of the Heart, Second Printing by Jill Downs
Battlenotes: Music of the Vietnam War by Lee Andresen
Color on the Land by Irene I.Luethge
Following in the Footsteps of Ernest Hemingway
      by Jay Ford Thurston
Hint of Frost, Essays on the Earth by Rusty King
Hometown Wisconsin by Marshall J. Cook
Potpourri From Kettle Land by Irene I. Luethge

FICTION

Burn Baby Burn by Mike Savage
Charleston Red by Sarah Galchus
Keeper of the Town short stories by Don Cameron
Lake Effect by Mike Savage
Lord of the Rinks by Mike Savage
Mining Sacred Ground by David Knop
Northern Lights Magic by Lori J. Glad
Off Season by Marshall J.Cook
Sailing Home by Lori J. Glad
Something in the Water by Mike Savage
Spirit of the Shadows by Rebel Sinclair
Summer Storm by Lori J. Glad
The Devil of Charleston by Rebel Sinclair
The Year of the Buffalo by Marshall J. Cook
Under the Rainbow by Jay Ford Thurston
Voices From the North Edge by St. Croix Writers

REGIONAL HISTORY, MEMOIR

A Life in Two Worlds by Betty Powell Skoog with Justine Kerfoot
Beyond the Freeway by Peter J. Benzoni
Crocodile Tears and Lipstick Smears by Fran Gabino
DakotaLand by Howard Jones
Fair Game by Fran Gabino
Memories of Iron River by Bev Thivierge
Stop in the Name of the Law by Alex O'Kash
Superior Catholics by Cheney and Meronek
Widow of the Waves by Bev Jamison

BUSINESS

Dare to Kiss the Frog by vanHauen, Kastberg & Soden
SoundBites, a Business Guide for Working With the Media
    Second Edition by Kathy Kerchner

POETRY

A Woman for All Time by Evelyn Gathman Haines
Eraser's Edge by Phil Sneve
Gleanings from the Hillsides by E.M. Johnson
In The Heart of the Forest by Diana Randolph
I Was Night by Bekah Bevins
Pathways by Mary B. Wadzinski
Philosophical Poems by E.M. Johnson
Poems of Faith and Inspiration by E.M. Johnson
Portrait of the Mississippi by Howard Jones
The Morning After the Night She Fell Into the Gorge
    by Heidi Howes
Thicker Than Water by Hazel Sangster
Treasures from the Beginning of the World by Jeff Lewis

HUMOR

Baloney on Wry by Frank Larson
Jackpine Savages by Frank Larson

OTHER BOOKS AVAILABLE FROM SP

Blueberry Summers by Lawrence Berube
Dakota Brave by Howard Jones
Spindrift Anthology by The Tarpon Springs Writer's Group

To order additional copies of

Journey into Joy
or
The Awakening of the Heart

Call

1-800-732-3867

or Email:

mail@savpress.com

You may purchase copies on-line at:

www.savpress.com
where
Visa/MC/Discover/American Express/Echeck
are accepted via PayPal